Remarkable Ham – The Untold Story

by Gordon Elsden

Gordon Elsden.

Written and published by
Gordon Elsden

Copyright © 2016

Layout and Artwork Production by Alison Graham
London Design Factory 020 8332 2432

ISBN 978 1 5272 0731 8

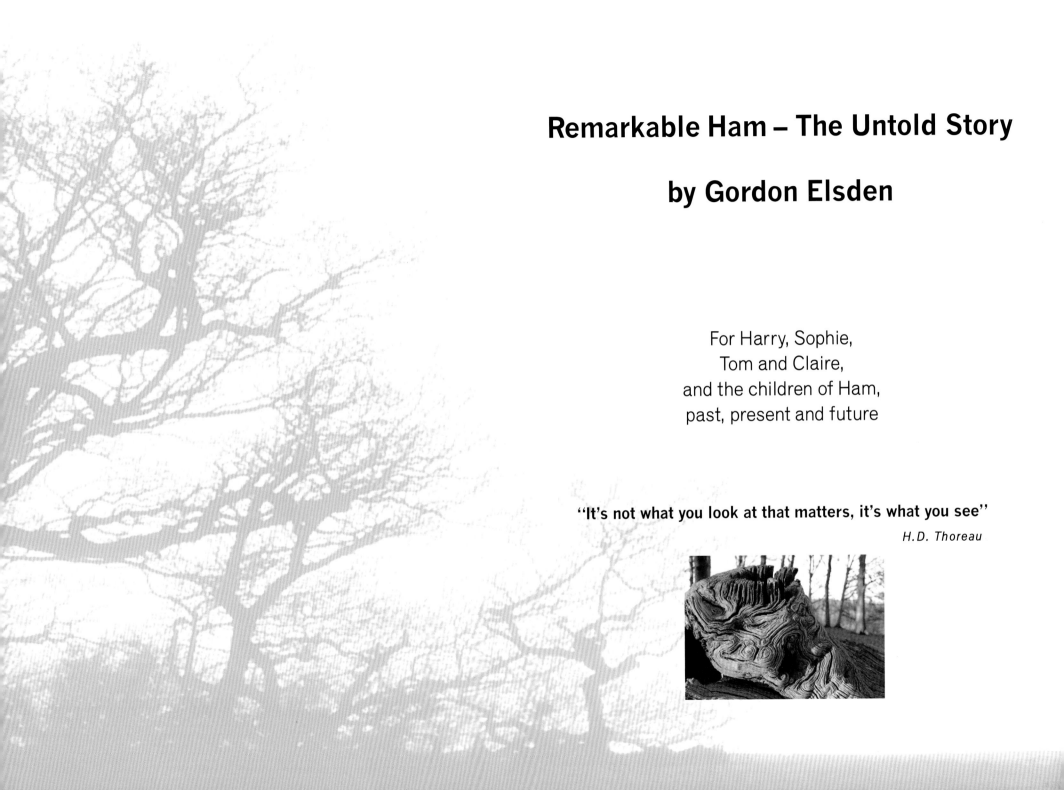

Remarkable Ham – The Untold Story

by Gordon Elsden

For Harry, Sophie,
Tom and Claire,
and the children of Ham,
past, present and future

"It's not what you look at that matters, it's what you see"

H.D. Thoreau

Remarkable Ham
The Untold Story

Written and published by
Gordon Elsden

Contents

Remarkable Ham – The Untold Story

Building the Story

Spending much of my life working in China and the Far East, I have come to genuinely appreciate my home in Ham, and the wonderful natural environment shaped by a meandering river, within a short walking distance from my front door.

Some four years ago I resolved to look a little closer at the history of Ham. I soon realised that there was very little to read before the relatively modern and very well documented Stuart period. So I set about the lengthy task of consolidating all of the known archaeological documents that cover Ham and also tracked down the numerous ancient artefacts from Ham that are stored in various museums including the British Museum and the Museum of London. I also consulted with acknowledged experts of the different periods. All this progressively enabled me to gain a better understanding of human activity in this area over many thousands of years.

Yet, I was also keen to put some flesh on the archaeological and historical bones and bring out the fascinating story of the people and the significant events that shaped their lives.

The narrative that unfolded and that forms this story is in many ways a microcosm of human existence. Many events featuring change and conflict in other parts of the world that we watch on TV screens from the comfort of our living rooms are likely to have taken place here in Ham at some stage in our own turbulent development.

Overview of the Story

Our story starts 60 million years ago when the area that we now know as Ham lay at the bottom of a warm tropical sea. It took another 20 million years for the ocean to recede and the land to emerge into the sunlight. Some 430,000 years ago a severe Ice Age pushed the River Thames further south to shape its meandering course around present day Ham.

The Thames has undoubtedly been the greatest single influence on the lives of the people living at Ham. As well as providing a great diversity of food, the river has served as a major artery for people, goods and ideas. It has also formed a natural physical and psychological boundary between Ham and the lands to the north. There is evidence that the people living alongside the river have also, at various times, revered the Thames as a sacred stream, an ancient portal to another world.

Lost to our common knowledge is a prehistoric settlement known as Coldharbour that served as a campsite in the Mesolithic age, and a settlement for people in the Neolithic age, the Bronze age, the Iron age and the Roman era. Ham also provided near Teddington Lock, one of the earliest Saxon settlements in England.

We have witnessed cycles of migration, displacement, population growth and decline as the local community has run the gauntlet of the depredations of warriors from rival communities and the Viking scourge in the Middle Saxon period. It is difficult to comprehend that communities in this area were terrorised by the prospect of being captured by raiders, enslaved and shipped overseas to strange lands, never to return.

Great armies marching west and north have cast their shadow over these lands. Stability, harmony and prosperity have been followed in turn by discord, conflict, chaos and decline, the seemingly never-ending cycle of human existence.

As the population increased, the people became more vulnerable to changes in the climate and failure of the crops. Until recently, a continuous shifting of the tidal head dramatically impacted on the wellbeing of riverside settlements. With more densely populated towns and settlements, people were increasingly susceptible to disease introduced from distant lands. Parts of the field systems in Richmond Park have lain deserted ever since

the Black Death ripped through the local farming communities.

Following the Norman invasion the fertile Manor of Ham was awarded by discerning Kings to various crusader Knights in recognition of their loyalty and service. The medieval Ham Manor Farm House survived the last five centuries only to be pulled down in 1958, along with its magnificent barn.

The Untold Story of Ham finishes where most local histories begin, with the building of Ham House and the enclosure of the land that would become Richmond Park. An unintended result of this has been the preservation within the Park of a medieval landscape – still there for us to explore and enjoy.

It is truly a remarkable story that needs to be told.

How to use this book

By dipping in and out of the chapters of the book, you will become acquainted with the fascinating events that have occurred here over many thousands of years. The two detailed maps at the beginning of the early chapters will provide you with a sense of the boundary of the ancient Parish of Ham and the location of the most interesting archaeological artefacts found within the landscape.

Armed with this knowledge, pluck yourselves (and maybe your children and grandchildren) from the comfort of your homes to go and engage with the natural landscape, much of which has been perfectly preserved. Feel the soil of this ancient land under your feet and pause to watch awhile the inexorable ebb and flow of the Thames River. There you can

consider the dramatic, fascinating, tangible and enlightening events that have preceded our own brief occupation of the land.

A deeper understanding of this special place where we live will also helpfully ensure that we take better care of it and preserve our precious **Legacy**.

Enjoy the Journey!
Gordon Elsden
Ham. April 2017

A coffee shop on Ham Parade where many of its curious and interested patrons helped inspire the telling of this story.

The Parish of Ham

1. Grey Court School
2. St Richard's Church and C of E Primary School
3. Meadlands Primary School
4. The Tiffin Girls' School
5. The Kingston Academy
6. Fern Hill Primary School
7. Latchmere School
8. St Agatha's Catholic Primary School
9. Saint Thomas Aquinas RC Church
10. Saint Andrew's Church
11. Thames Young Mariners Base
12. YMCA Hawker Centre
13. The New Inn
14. The Hand & Flower
15. The Ham Brewery Tap
16. Site of the Old Lodge
17. St. Peter's Church

The red circles with numbers show the route of the Beating of the Bounds annual pilgrimage detailed in the text of this chapter

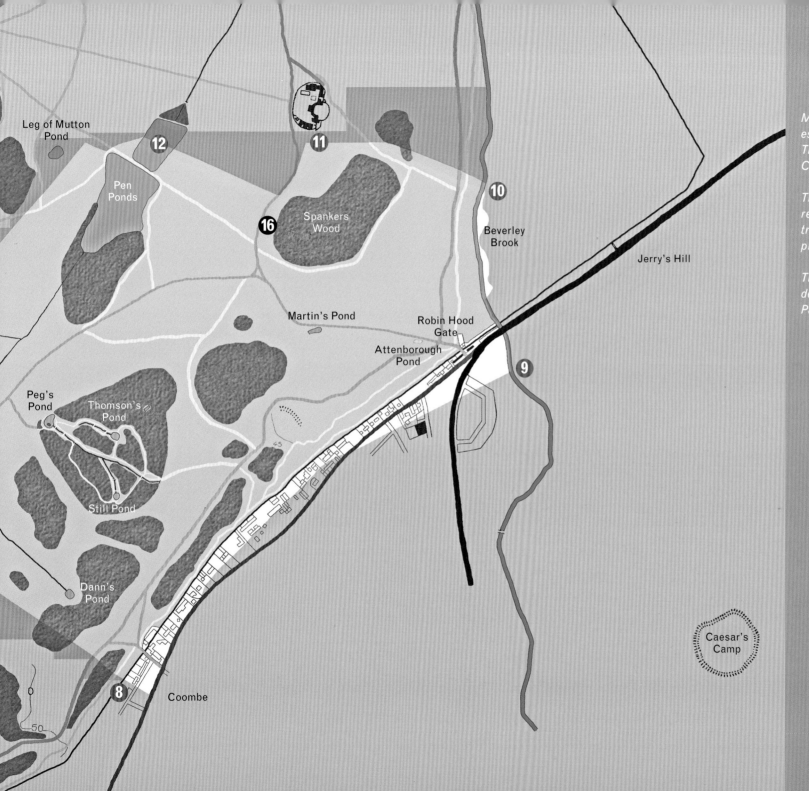

Leg of Mutton
Pond

12

Pen
Ponds

16

Spankers
Wood

11

10

Beverley
Brook

Martin's Pond

Robin Hood
Gate

Attenborough
Pond

9

Peg's
Pond

Thomson's
Pond

Still Pond

Dann's
Pond

Coombe

8

Jerry's Hill

Caesar's
Camp

*Map of the Parish of Ham
established from the 1841
Tithe map drawn by Thomas
Crawter.*

*The original map accurately
recorded every field, road,
track, building, garden and
plantation within the Parish.*

*The shaded area clearly
defines the border of the
Parish.*

Beating the Bounds

PLAN
of the
PARISH of HAM
in the
County of Surrey
Compiled from the Original Plans of the
SEVERAL PROPRIETORS
BY
Thomas Crawter of Cobham
1841

Scale three Chains to an Inch

Ancient Ham

In times gone by Ham covered a far larger area than it does today. In 1841 Thomas Crawter of Cobham, painstakingly drew a tithe map to accurately record every field, road, building, garden and plantation within the Parish of Ham.(2) The layout of the fields and the boundary of the parish had changed little since mediaeval times which means that the map provides us with a very accurate picture of ancient Ham. This map, so painstakingly drawn, will serve to define Ham for the purpose of this story.

There was once a stretch of land where modern day Ham now lies and not a lot happened for a very long time. But then, a mighty river, bolstered with billions of gallons of melt-water, rock and ice, changed its course and violently gouged out a deep valley in the land.

And everything changed!

Ham is inextricably linked with the River Thames. The river shaped the landscape of Ham and has provided abundant resources to the people who, for thousands of years, have been drawn to its fertile and very desirable environment. The river has served as an essential artery for people, goods and ideas. At times it has been considered a sacred stream, a portal to a spiritual domain. The river has defined the character of Ham and throughout human existence here, it has provided a physical and psychological boundary.

Its people considered the relationship between the river and the land and gave it the name Hamm or Ham meaning *"land that is contained within the bend of a river"* (1)

Beating the Bounds of the Parish on Ascension day

Beating the Bounds, Beating the Boys

For a villager living in England many years ago, the bounds of his village were the most important bounds that he knew. The "Beating the Bounds" practice dates from Anglo-Saxon times but may incorporate pagan rituals from earlier times. The beat was intended to reconfirm the boundaries of the Parish to the residents, and most importantly to remind neighbouring residents of the limits of their own land and therefore discourage any encroachment.

On the 40th day of Easter (Ascension day), the local priest and older members of the parish would lead the younger boys on a walk of the bounds to show them clearly the exact location of the boundary with other parishes and to pray for a good harvest. Armed with thin branches of willow or birch, the elder parishioners would beat the boundary markers that were located on trees or large stones. On occasions the younger boys were also whipped or had their heads bumped against the boundary markers, to ensure that the memory of their exact location was not forgotten! (3)

These ancient boundaries have long since been forgotten by the majority of the residents of Ham and Kingston but thanks to the endeavours of Thomas Crawter we can set the record straight and re-establish the "bounds" of the Parish of St Andrew's on the modern urban landscape of Ham.

St Andrew's Church at the heart of the Parish of Ham

Sir Richard Owen, the first Director of the Natural History Museum. The man who created the term Dinosaur and did much to define natural prehistory is buried in St Andrew's Church in Ham. Pictured standing next to a Moa skeleton

The Boundary of the Parish of Ham

The main North South axis of the Parish of Ham is the Richmond/Upper Ham Road but the Parish in earlier times also encompassed a significant part of what is now Richmond Park and the Robin Hood Lands either side of the London to Kingston turnpike (now A308), past Robin Hood Gate. A small hamlet known as Hatch was located on the north side of the Common including the New Inn. (4) Ironically the Parish of Ham does not include Ham House as this falls within the Parish of Petersham.

Starting just to the west of Ham House at the edge of the River Thames (*Location 1 on the map*) the Ham boundary heads south running

The boundary follows the river further south through the Lock named Teddington despite the fact that both the lock and its lock house are located on the southern Surrey side of the river in Ham. *(3)*

along the middle of the Thames. The beaters would ritually row up the middle of the river beating the water on either side. They would soon pass a farmstead known as Coldharbour, which has long since disappeared but was located around the current site of the Thames Young Mariners Base. *(location 2)*

Coldharbour with its adjacent fields was the location of a number of different settlements throughout the prehistoric period, the remaining evidence of which was injudiciously dug up when gravel became a more attractive commercial proposition to the Earl of Dysart.

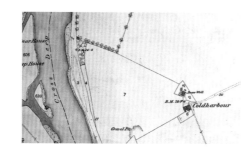

The boundary continues past the YMCA sports centre and fields, past Half Mile tree (now a Horse Chestnut) *(4)* located where Lower Ham Road meets the river until, just after Albany Park Canoe & Sailing Centre, a small white boundary stone *(5)*, marks the boundary with Kingston. The boundary then heads directly east, crosses the Richmond road, passes through the grounds of The Kingston Academy and Fern Hill Primary School then makes a series of doglegs (originally following the edges of fields) past the south end of Latchmere Lane round the Latchmere recreation ground, formerly the Latchmere meadow, into Latchmere Road. It passes the front of Latchmere School then once more follows the edges of long forgotten fields to the junction of Park Road and Tudor Drive (6), before continuing up the northern end of Park Road towards Barnfield Riding Centre. It then heads directly east crossing the wall into Richmond Park and cuts up through the Thatched House enclosure (7) running north of the main house.

From here it heads in a south-easterly direction to just south of Ladderstile gate (8) before crossing the current park boundary and the Kingston Hill Road. It then tracks the original London to Portsmouth Road (A308) past Robin Hood gate to the Beverley Brook (9). The original Parish of Ham included both this section of the Turnpike coming out of London and the Robin Hood Inn which was an important staging post for the horse drawn coaches making their way to Portsmouth via Kingston and which had to change their team of horses every eight to ten miles. At the end of the 18th century this section of the road running onto Putney Heath was the frequent of a notorious Kingston-born highwayman, Jerry Abershaw.

Unlike Robin Hood, he and his fellow highwaymen pursued both rich and poor with equal vigour and several Ham residents were made to "Stand and deliver". After killing

an officer of the law, Abershaw was finally apprehended and hanged. To serve as a warning to his fellow highwaymen, his body was suspended in an iron cage swinging below a gibbet overlooking the highway, until the crows picked his bones clean! (5) Now, his image on the sign at Tibbet's corner looks down every day on thousands of unaware drivers negotiating the lesser peril of slow moving traffic.

Above: An ancient drive just north of Thatched House connecting Ham Cross with what is now Ladderstile gate and used for driving cattle in Mediaeval times

Left: Jerry's Hill gibbet!

Far left: Image of Jerry Abershaw at Tibbet's Corner

The Beverley Brook forms a natural boundary with the Parish of Putney. The brook enters the park and the Parish of Ham near Robin Hood Gate. Here Beavers once made their home, hence the name Beverley meaning beaver but records show that they have been extinct in Britain since the twelfth century (6). Nevertheless, the stream is abundantly full of thriving trout, most easily seen from the wooden bridge near Roehampton Lodge.

The boundary briefly follows the course of the brook *(10)* heading north on the way to the Thames, then turns directly west to climb between Spankers Wood and White Lodge *(11)*. Continuing west, the boundary cuts though the middle of the smaller of the Pen Ponds *(12)*, which required an unfortunate and probably young beater to swim across.

Looking back across the vast grassy plain to the edge of Spankers Wood you can make out the distinctive shape of a Cedar of Lebanon tree. This sentinel of the past overlooks the site of the Old Lodge, a grandiose weekend hunting retreat used by the Prime Minister, Sir Robert Walpole from about 1727 to his death in 1745. (The Old Lodge was built on the site of Hartleton Farm). Sir Robert and George II would often hunt together and it is said that the closing of the House of Commons on Saturdays was due to Robert Walpole's habitual weekend hunting in the Park. Around this time the King built New Lodge, now known as White Lodge.

Old lodge was demolished in the 1840's and apart from the Cedar of Lebanon, there remains no trace of its presence.

The boundary now heads west across the open plain of the park past White Ash Lodge. It then crosses the park road running between Kingston and Richmond gates *(13)* before dropping down the hill to cut through the current Sudbrook golf course as far as the Upper Ham Road. It is important to remember that the boundary which followed field boundaries was well established before Richmond Park, Pen Ponds and the golf course were created! Reaching the Upper Ham Road, the boundary with Petersham is marked by a small white stone just opposite a house called "The Poplars"*(14)*. Just next to the Poplars on the Petersham side was the small Wesleyan chapel where Van Gogh gave a sermon in November 1876.

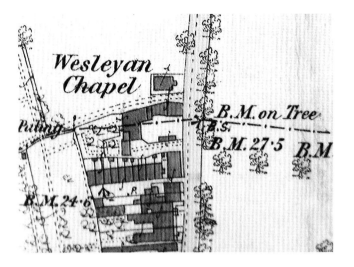

Left: 1880 Map showing the Ham boundary crossing the Petersham Road and the small chapel where Van Gogh gave a sermon in 1876

Far left bottom: The ancient tithe barn of Ham

Below: Grey Court House

Heading directly west the boundary crosses the avenue leading from Ham Common to Ham House then makes a sharp turn to the north, running just east of Ham Street.

A Forgotten Manor

Top: Ham Manor Farm later known as Hatch Farm then Secrett's Farm after the tenant farmers.
Charlotte Hatch is standing outside with her husband Edward Rayne. (of Rayne's Park) Circa 1870
Above: Photos of Ham Manor Farm taken in 1956. The Almshouses in Ham Street opposite the present day
library are clearly shown on the map and serve to identify the location of the original farm buildings

Just west of Ham Street was located the original Mediaeval Manor House dating from the 1400s (15). It predated Ham House by nearly 200 years. It was undoubtedly an archaeological treasure trove but unfortunately, along with the ancient barn the Manor house was demolished in 1958 to make way for a precinct of shops on the corner of Ashburnam Road and Ham Street, opposite Grey Court school (7).

In September 1805 a small boy, John Henry Newman, was living in Grove House in Ham (later Grey Court House part of Grey Court School). On the 10th day of this month, Admiral Lord Nelson was a guest at White Lodge, located just north of the boundary with Ham in Richmond Park. Following dinner he explained to Lord Sidmouth his intended plan of attack against the French Fleet, by drawing lines on the table with a wine-moistened finger.

Several weeks later Nelson was dead and the young John Henry Newman lay in bed entranced by the candles placed in the windows of Grove House to celebrate the victory at Trafalgar. For the remainder of his life Cardinal John Newman looked back on his time at Ham as the happiest period of his childhood.

Continuing north past the former Royal Oak Pub (16) the beaters would have passed through the extensive grounds of Ham House. Ham House was not part of the Manor of Ham but is located in Petersham, though the restaurant and coffee shop in the Orangery (17) with its surrounding gardens and stable block can be warmly claimed by Ham!

The trek finally brings the beaters back to their starting point at the bank of the Thames. Finishing at dusk, this would undoubtedly have been a long and tiring "Beating of the bounds" especially for those who were getting an occasional thrashing along the way!

The Beginning of the Story

This opening chapter has served to exhaustively track the ancient boundary of Ham and define the full extent of the Parish, far larger than is commonly recognised. With this done, the journey into the very distant past and the telling of the story of the land and its synergy with the people who acknowledged its vitality can now begin.

The Thames shapes Ham

A Tropical Ocean

Forty million years ago, as ice sheets developed in the Antarctic and Arctic regions, locking up vast amounts of water, the seas gradually receded and the land of current day Ham first emerged into the sunlight. The land formed a

Sixty million years ago the area, which is now known as Ham, lay below a warm tropical ocean. (1) Over millions of years, tiny particles of eroded rock were carried by rivers and deposited in the sea and lagoons close to the coast. (2) These particles were combined with the deposits from ancient marine creatures including sharks, molluscs and sea snails and diverse tropical plants such as palms, climbers, magnolias and mangroves. The resulting bluish-brown mash, commonly known as London Clay, progressively built up to form the underlying soil of the London Thames Valley region. (3)

Left: Mangroves bordering a tropical lagoon some 50 million years ago. Artist's impression of how our environment may have appeared at this time based on evidence from plant and animal remains.

Far left: Megalodon

Right: Sea shell fossil found in the Richmond area

Top: An ice sheet covering the land

natural basin, ideal for the Thames, some time later, to find an alternative route to the sea. (4)

Meanwhile, the Thames river system was beginning to form some distance to the north of its current course. By about three million years before present (BP) the river had forged a valley near St. Albans and entered a dry basin, now the North Sea, near Harwich. Here it flowed in a north westerly direction until it merged with the ancestor of the Modern Rhine. (1)

Understanding the impact of the Ice Ages

It is important to recognise that the climate of Southern Britain has fluctuated widely during the last two million years. This land has experienced extremes from a temperate sub-tropical climate when hippos wallowed in warm rivers to arctic conditions, which rendered the land inhospitable to human beings. The term Ice Age is therefore a little confusing in that it really refers to a period of time during which there were alternating phases of cooler and warmer temperatures.

We are currently living in a warmer phase of the Quaternary period, which began about 2.58 million years ago, the last of five known Ice Ages on Earth.

At this time, permanent slabs of ice up to several kilometers deep (but referred to as ice sheets) developed in Antarctica and Greenland. During cooler (glacial) periods the ice sheets would advance further south and during warmer (interglacial) periods they would retreat. This had a dramatic impact on the climate. During glacial periods, with so much water locked up in the ice sheets, rainfall was only half of what we receive today and the sea level dropped by as much as 100 metres, making land accessible between continents and islands.

Fast moving winds swept the debris of the barren tundra, creating immense dust storms. Current sea levels are high compared with the average over the last million years and for most of the history of this land it would have been possible to walk from Continental Europe to Britain without fear of getting your feet wet! (5)

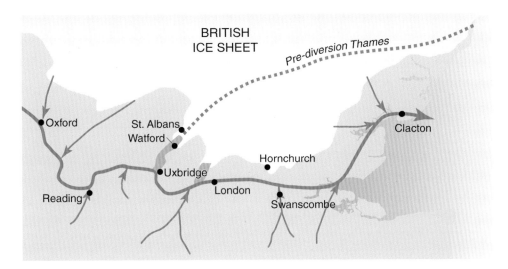

A River comes to Ham

The diversion of the Thames to its current course

By about 430,000 years Before Present (BP), an extreme Ice Age known as the Anglian, buried England, north of Watford, beneath a huge slab of ice, up to 1000 feet deep (6). With available water locked up in immense glaciers, the ocean withdrew, to expose the bed of what is now the North Sea.

The destructive southward advance of the ice sheet now forced the course of the original Thames further south into an alternative

basin leading to the sea. As a result a new river valley was cut through the soft clay. This would be recognisable today as the course of the modern Thames that loops round Ham, though the surrounding terrain would still require some moulding and the addition of a few people!

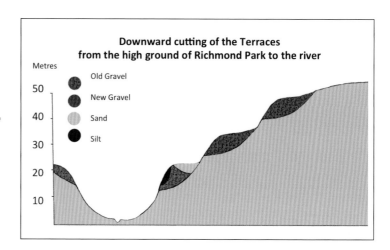

**Downward cutting of the Terraces
from the high ground of Richmond Park to the river**

Metres

Old Gravel
New Gravel
Sand
Silt

50
40
30
20
10

Building the Terraces downwards

Modern day images of a meandering tranquil Thames are far removed from the violence that surrounded the early development of the modern river. As global air temperatures increased, the glaciers began to melt and in turn released huge volumes of water, fractured ice and the remnants of crushed rock and flint released from the chalk. This maelstrom of melt water, ice, rock and sand gouged its way down to the low lying sea, grinding a deep channel through the soft clay and depositing the heavier sand, huge quantities of gravel and deposits of rich river mud known as alluvium at the edges of the river throughout its length.

As the glaciers melted away, and the sea level rose, the Thames settled into a broad, shallow and meandering river with water flowing more slowly throughout its course to the sea. In many sections the channel was braided, with many more islands and sandbanks. In prehistoric times there were probably several aits (eyots) in the Thames between Twickenham and Ham although only two survive today, the largest of which is Eel Pie Island (7).

The river would have been considerably wider than the channeled Thames that we see today. An excavation in 1994 at the former British Aerospace site (now the Hawker Estate) between the river and Richmond Road records the following (8):

"Floodplain sand and gravel was cut by several undated features filled with alluvium, including small gullies and at least one large channel over 100m wide. The latter was approximately parallel to the River Thames and may once have formed part of the braided course of this river."

Each successive melting of the ice sheets and subsequent flood gouged anew the riverbed, cutting deeper and deeper into the soft London Clay, and depositing gravel, silt and sand at the edge of the river (9).

During the last deep freeze, fine deposits of soil known as brick earth, which is the principal component of London's brick buildings, were carried by the wind from the floodplains down over the lower terraces of the Thames valley (4).

Combined with a gradual elevation of the land driven by tectonic uplift, the terraces of gravel were progressively built downwards from the higher ground (10). In this way the current landscape of Richmond Park and Ham was gradually shaped.

In the area of Ham, the river gravels capped with the rich brick earth were to prove relatively fertile and later became intensively settled throughout the prehistoric period. Furthermore the deposits of river mud known as alluvium were ideal for the growth of rich pasture land adjacent to the river.

Continuous Movement and Erosion

The law of gravity determines that the higher the sea level, the slower the flow of the river water to the sea. With a high sea level, a meandering or braiding river develops with the river snaking its way back and forth down the valley. The water is forced into a spiral as it rounds each bend resulting in the erosion of the bank on the outside of each meander loop. At the same time, sediment is deposited on the inside of each loop and over time the loop progressively becomes more concave. In this way the river channel and flood plain are continually being reshaped and this is how the river at Ham has evolved its course (11).

At a later time, any riverside human settlements on the outside of meander curves at Kingston, Teddington and Richmond might reasonably be expected to

Step into Ham

become eroded into the river. Conversely sites at Ham, Twickenham and West Molesey may find themselves further inland (10).

Inhabiting the Land

With the Thames having roughly settled its route to the sea, the increasingly fertile and abundant landscape at Ham was now ready for the arrival of grazing animals, and the predators and humans that hunted them. But these early humans, were not humans as we know them!

Prehistoric Ham

Locations of where some of the most interesting pre-historic and ancient artefacts have been found.

1 Lower Palaeolithic hand axe 400,000 BP

2 Coldharbour site, Upper Palaeolithic, Mesolithic, Neolithic, Bronze Age and Iron Age artefacts found

3 Maize fields, Mesolithic flints

4 Ham Dip Pond, Mesolithic flints

5 Thames foreshore, Mesolithic mace head

6 Isabella Plantation Neolithic flint axe 7,000 BP

7 Parkleys, Neolithic arrow heads

8 Ham Gate, Neolithic ground axe

9 Neolithic Long Barrow

10 Aubrey's Ramp

11 Bronze Age sword found in the Thames

12 Half mile tree, Bronze Age dagger and other artifacts found in the Thames nearby

13 Coombe, Bronze Age workshops

14 Iron Age Hill Fort

15 Iron Age Hill Fort (Caesar's Camp)

16 Iron Age and Roman pottery, glass bottles

17 Iron Age coins

18 Cinerary urn of Roman period

19 Early Saxon settlement

20 Saxon sword, shield, spear
and Christian pendant

21 Saxon Chapel

22 Middle Saxon settlement

23 Mediaeval Manor House

24 Ancient Track

Jerry's Hill

Coombe

Predators

The Nature of the Environment at Ham

In 430,000 BP, towards the end of the Anglian glaciation, Southern England experienced a warmer climate enabling mixed deciduous woodlands and grass floodplains to flourish. The Thames, while meandering through a wide flood plain, supported dolphins, pike, salmon and perch. Beavers occupied the riverbank and Ospreys patrolled the skies (1). The forests supported a growing population of wild boar, red deer, fallow deer, macaque monkeys, aurochsen, and bear which would occasionally venture out onto the grass-bearing floodplains to cautiously drink and feed alongside large herds of horse, straight-tusked elephant and rhino. These animals were hunted by the top predators of the time, including wolves, lions and an early species of human known as *homo heidelbergensis*, the predecessor of both the Neanderthals in Europe and our species of Homo sapiens evolving out of Africa (2).

Early Humans passing through Ham
(location 1 on the map)

The oldest artefacts discovered within the Parish of Ham were found in Richmond Park east of White Lodge. These comprised a hand axe on the surface of the gravel and a fragment of a rolled flake found in a trench nearby. They date from the Lower Palaeolithic period (about 400,000 BC) and are among the earliest Palaeolithic material found in Surrey (2).

Several hand axes have also been found in the bed of the Thames at various locations between Kingston, Richmond, Kew and Putney. They were in a very rolled condition suggesting that they started their life in one of the higher terraces but were then rolled from one gravel terrace to another over time (2).

Above: Lower Palaeolithic hand axe dating from 400,000 BP found east of White Lodge in Richmond Park

Left: A reconstruction drawing of a Palaeolithic straight-tusked elephant

Far left: A reconstruction drawing of a Palaeolithic woolly rhino

Prehistoric – belonging to times before history was written down. So history in Britain only commenced with the arrival of the Romans in AD 43.

The Nature of the early Humans passing through Ham

Fossils of these early people found in the south of England have shown a close physical resemblance to modern day humans, though somewhat more hairy. Evidence from the Boxgrove site just outside Chichester indicates that they killed the larger animals themselves as well as scavenging from other predators, possibly using spears

Right: Homo heidelbergensis shaping a hand axe in the land that is now Richmond Park some 400,000 years ago

Below: Around 300,000 years ago, Hominins butchering a brown bear and fending off other predators on the Thames river bank

shaped out of wood. It also indicates that they comprehensively butchered large animals using carefully worked flint hand axes (3).

Their ability to hunt as an organised group with the necessary skill to drive other predators away from the kill and then keep them away positioned them at the top of the food chain. It is believed that they operated in sustainable groups, numbering around fifty in size. A proficiency in reading the landscape gave them a distinct advantage when sourcing material for their tools and weapons as well as the hunting of their prey (4).

In addition to a diet of protein rich meat these people, living in crude shelters close to the Thames, would also have collected plant food including fruit and nuts. As the climate was colder than it is today it is likely that they would have made additional clothing from the furs and skins of the animals that they had butchered (5).

Over the next 310,000 years until 70,000 BP the climate of Britain fluctuated between the extremes of glacial arctic conditions and more temperate climates and for much of this time Humans were absent from Britain.

An African Climate and Landscape in Ham

Perhaps the most famous fossils, not too far from Ham, are the remains of Hippopotamus found during excavations in Trafalgar Square. These, along with other bones of elephants, rhinos, wild oxen, red deer, fallow deer, lions and hyena were dated to approximately 100,000 years BP. Insects included dung beetles, cockchafers, weevils and water beetles. Pollen spores identified a variety of grasses, hazel, maple, hawthorn and water chestnut (5). The Thames at this time would have been a swiftly flowing river with hippopotamus wallowing in marshy areas at the river's edge surrounded by rushes with a surrounding landscape of open grassland.

The warmer climate also tends to suggest that Britain during this period was separated from the Continent.

Left: Representation of the Thames during an interglacial period 125,000 to 90,000 BP

Below: Neanderthal hunters stalk woolly mammoths across the Thames Valley tundra 50,000 years ago

Neanderthals pass through Ham

Neanderthals that had evolved from *homo heidelbergensis*, reappeared in Britain around 60,000 years ago. The environment at Ham at this time was hostile with treeless tundra and temperatures averaging 13 degrees C in the summer and -10 degrees C in the winter. With this marked change in climate, sea levels fell and a land bridge with Europe was re-established.

Though somewhat shorter and stockier in stature than their predecessors they possessed great upper body strength. Neanderthals hunted reindeer, horse and on occasions mammoth and woolly rhinoceros. This was an extremely dangerous pursuit resulting often in serious injury and death. Analysis of the remains of Neanderthal people in England suggests that they incurred injuries comparable to a modern day cowboy riding bulls in rodeos (6). Their hunting expeditions invariably finished at close range using stone tipped spears.

Evidence of Neanderthal presence in Ham
(location 2)

A broken and rolled spearhead dating from around 40,000 BP was found in one of the gravel pits near the Coldharbour settlement in Ham (7). This is now on display at the Museum of London. Notes at the Museum propose that this spearhead may be a Neanderthal copy of a Homo-sapien spearhead. The Neanderthals co-existed with Homo-sapiens for thousands of years (8).

Far left: A mammoth tooth found in the Thames in Richmond

Left: Upper Palaeolithic spearhead dating from 40.000 BP found near the Coldharbour settlement in Ham. A Neanderthal copy!

Above: This artist's impression shows a mammoth being separated from the herd and forced into boggy ground. Mammoths lived in Europe for over 4 million years. They finally died out at the end of the last Ice Age around 10,000 years ago

Artist's reconstruction of how our land would have appeared about 40,000 years ago based on evidence of fossil, mammal, plant and insect remains found in a gravel pit near Isleworth. In the foreground is Beverley Brook. The treeless landscape supports bison, reindeer and brown bear

The arrival of the Homo sapiens (intelligent humans)

Homo sapiens, our direct ancestors, arrived in Britain about 45,000 years ago. They brought with them a more sophisticated range of flint tools and the ability to shape bone, antler and wood. This marked the beginning of the Upper Palaeolithic age, which lasted for 33,000 years (2). Although they were hunter-gatherers, the severe climate deterred them from settling in Britain. It is believed that they crossed the land bridge connecting the Continent to England to hunt large game during the warmer summer months. Even then, the landscape and climate was far from comfortable. Their main quarry would have been tundra-loving herbivores such as mammoth, bison, horse and reindeer. Following the course of the river up stream they would have passed through Ham.

A diversity of Mammals

Animal bones, plant and molluscan remains which indicated marshy ground associated with a slow moving stream have been found in gravel deposits at Popes Grove in Twickenham some 400 meters west of the Thames. Subsequent identification of hundreds of animal bones found here disclosed reindeer, wild boar, red deer, roe deer, wolf and bison. The marrow bones of the bison had been split and cracked, possibly indicating the presence of humans.

In the 1950s about 2km to the north of Ham in gravel pits in Isleworth, plant fragments were discovered along with bones belonging to reindeer, bison, mammoth and woolly rhinoceros. These have been radio carbon dated to around 43,140 BP (9).

A reconstruction drawing of an Upper Palaeolithic reindeer

The Devensian Deep Freeze (known as the last glacial maximum)

Around 25,000 BP a sudden deteriorating climate resulted in the disappearance of all the animals and plants that the Neanderthals were familiar with. Unable to adapt to the new environment they became extinct. Homo-sapiens, meanwhile, simply left Britain and headed south to a warmer and more supportive climate (8).

Yet the Neanderthals did not completely disappear. Genetic studies have disclosed that the modern human in Europe has traces of Neanderthal DNA which indicates that there was a degree of interbreeding between our ancestors and the Neanderthals (8). By 16,000 BP an ice sheet extended over the north of England and the Midlands. With so much water locked up in the ice sheets, the sea level fell by up to 150 metres. The huge weight of the ice covering Britain compressed the top surface of the land and throughout its length crushed surface rocks into small fragments (5).

It was during this period that the deposits of fine soil known as brickearth were carried by the wind from the floodplains to cover the lower terraces of the Thames Valley including Ham and Twickenham (5).

As temperatures increased at the end of the Ice Age some 12,000 years ago, the melted water caused the sea level to rise and the released weight of the ice slab allowed the land to slowly spring back. The channel of the Thames was now gouged to its deepest recorded level by the ensuing melt water, ice and crushed rock (2).

So modern humans now find themselves 12,000 years into the ensuing interglacial (warm) period. Yet the previous interglacial period lasted 20,000 years and the one prior to that lasted 140,000 years.

Prehistoric Time Table		
Lower Palaeolithic	1,000,000 BP	to 350,000 BP
Middle Palaeolithic	350,000 BP	to 45,000 BP
Upper Palaeolithic	45,000 BP	to 12,000 BP
Mesolithic	10,000 BC	to 4,000 BC
Neolithic	4,000 BC	to 2,500 BC
Copper Age	2,500 BC	to 2,200 BC
Bronze Age	2,200 BC	to 700 BC
Iron Age	700 BC	to 42 AD

Ultimate Hunters

The Mesolithic Period from 10,000 BC to 4000 BC

The Landscape

By 10,000 BC the climate in Ham became comparable to the weather that we experience today. The birch trees, which had replaced the tundra forests of fir, died within a relatively short period of time but played an essential role in both enriching the earth and providing shelter for more durable species of tree. Following this pattern, immense woodlands of deciduous oak, elm, hazel and lime steadily filled the landscape while alder established a presence on the riverbanks. Exactly the same process is happening today in Ham Common Woods, where you can see the carcasses of decaying silver birch lying beneath the canopy of oak trees.

The dense forests and fertile riverside landscape now increasingly supported edible plants and provided good habitation for red and roe deer and aurochs which had progressively replaced the large herds of horse and reindeer of the open tundra and grasslands.

> Mesolithic (Greek)
> Meso - middle
> Lithos - stone
> hence "middle stone age"

Humans in Ham during the Mesolithic Period
(location 2)

It would appear that the Thames riverbank, especially at Ham, was an area particularly favoured by nomadic hunters. The environment of Ham provided congenial living conditions, supporting richer vegetation, a high density and variety of wild animals and birds, and in the river an abundance of fish including salmon and eels (1).

Individual hunters or small groups equipped with bow and arrow and flint tipped spears stealthily pursued red deer, aurochs and wild boar through the forests and otter and beaver along the riverbanks. Stealth, patience and cunning had become essential requirements of the hunter over and above brute strength and raw courage. Humans were gradually learning how to make their life easier. Wolves and bear were competing predators and, though unlikely to be a direct threat to groups of humans, they would have proved a continual nuisance.

An imaginary reconstruction of a band of hunters stalking red deer in a clearing in natural woodland around 9000 BP

Reconstruction of an early Mesolithic settlement

The optimum size of a group was now 25 people with accomplished hunter gatherers exerting themselves on average, 4 to 5 hours a day.

The nomadic community that used Ham as a base is likely to have worked in rotation a number of designated camps that provided good hunting and had easy access to nutritional plants. As soon as they had exploited the food resources in a given area, they moved on to another. Coldharbour would have been a preferred base during the summer when there was less risk of flooding from the river. (location 2) During the winter the community may have moved to the higher ground of the upper terraces in Richmond Park and Wimbledon Common venturing down to the river as and when they needed to fish. Shelter would have consisted of basic structures such as tents made of animal hide or huts made from wood and sealed with reeds.

Evidence from other sites indicates that the group's activity is likely to have centred on elevated ground above the river flood line, and around a hearth which provided both heat and security. Around this the members of the group would have made axes and other flint tools, worked antlers and prepared hides. While so engaged they would have chatted amongst themselves and told stories (3).

With a lower water level and a braided channel, the river at Ham was likely to have been fordable (1).

This would have made it an ideal location to trap fish including salmon and eels; waterfowl and the smaller mammals of the river such as beaver. Shallow draught canoes and kayaks travelling up and down the river would probably have had to be hauled up on shore at Ham and carried overland to bypass the shallows. This therefore made Ham a suitable stopping place (1).

The gravel islands or "eyots" such as Eel Pie Island in the midst of the marshy Thames would also have

been ideal places to fish or set traps for birds (4).

Unlike later tools and weapons made of bronze and iron, which decayed in a relatively short time, flint tools have endured throughout the ages. Although their makers and users are long since gone, their story can be told through the tools that they left behind. Sharp edged flint flakes, scrapers, saws and adzes were used to butcher and skin game, carve antlers, shape wood and hollow out tree trunks to make log boats.

29

Location of Mesolithic Artefacts found in the Ham Area
(location 2)

With the relatively recent urbanisation of Ham, we are fortunate that a number of archaeologists took a great interest in the prehistoric history of Ham at the end of the 19th Century and beginning of the 20th and assiduously collected and documented as many artefacts as they could find.

David Field, an acknowledged Surrey Archeologist recorded that the major site for the archaeologists locating flint implements was around Coldharbour (near the current location of Thames Young Mariners base), alongside and sometimes astride a gravel bank that ran parallel to the river. This was probably an embankment, which may have provided a degree of shelter [1].

Field was of the opinion that the site at Coldharbour was ideal for a settlement and that it has seen almost continuous though perhaps intermittent occupation from the early prehistoric periods to the present day [1].

Several other prominent archaeologists, Johnson & Wright (end of the 19th Century), Edwards (early 1900's), Marsden (1930's), Wymer (1949) and Lacaille (1966), collected material from around the Coldharbour site, retaining only the better samples, while other collectors such as Knowles (1910) purchased artefacts directly from local people and gravel diggers [1].

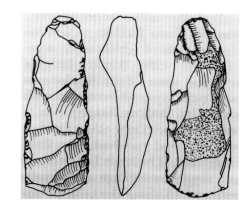

Left: A rare tool found near Coldharbour. It appears to be a hoe or mattock used for digging or loosening soil

Right: Reconstruction showing how a stone axe could have been attached to a wooden handle

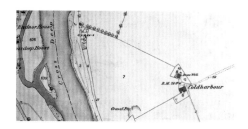

Numerous Mesolithic flint implements and much waste material has been collected from the area around Coldharbour. This includes adzes, awls, scrapers, blades and a total of eighteen axes, most with tranchet edges, which are characteristic of the Mesolithic age. The large number of axes found at Coldharbour tends to suggest that the site was also used for boat construction and maintenance [1].

Left: OS Map of 1880 showing the location of Coldharbour. See location 2 on the Prehistoric Ham map

An adze is a multi purpose tool used for smoothing or carving wood.

An awl is a long pointed spike generally used for piercing or marking materials.

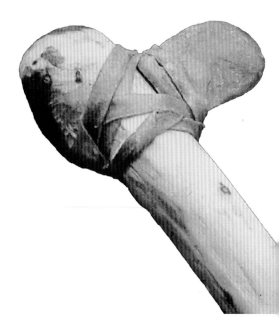

The variety of waste material indicates that flints were being shaped on site. Furthermore, the presence of a high concentration of good quality Downs flint indicates that the Ham site was of sufficient importance and stability for material to be regularly transported down from the North Downs (1).

Also practiced at Ham was the more advanced technique of manufacturing microliths (small stones) for making the heads of bone or wooden spears as well as arrowheads. Lacaille believed that the relics from Ham dating from 8000 BP "constitute a comprehensive and representative clutch of artefacts and exhibited a high level of skill in their making."(2).

Field commented; "Mesolithic settlement of which Ham was a typical settlement was relatively intense along this stretch of river."(5). The riverside environment at Ham and other sites along this part of the river, were so attractive to humans during this period, that they would have supported a relatively high percentage of the human population of the south of England!

Altogether there are 13 major concentrations of core Mesolithic tools recovered from the river between Kingston and Battersea, at approximate intervals of 1.5 miles. Apart from Ham no sites have been found on adjacent banks (5). This is probably because these settlements were on the outside of meander curves and over time eroded away by the snaking river. Ham conversely was on the inside of the curve and this is why most of the finds have been located 100 to 200 yards from the river.

Other Mesolithic Material was found in:

- Maize fields closer to Ham Street (location 3)

- Forbes House on Ham Common

- Tudor Drive

- The land leading to Richmond Park (6)

- The Thames foreshore near Ham House (location 5)

- The site of Walkers Farm (now Parkleys) (location 7)

This shows a direct link between the River edge at Coldharbour and the upper terraces of Richmond Park where there is also considerable evidence of Mesolithic occupation.

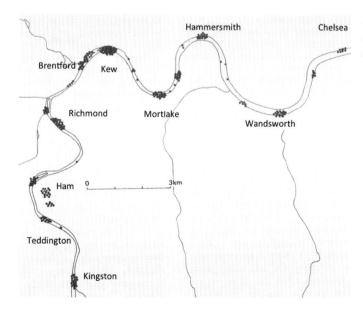

Left: Distribution of Mesolithic core tools in West London

The land of Richmond Park is well endowed with natural springs occurring even on the high ground. In prehistoric times it would have been covered with light heath vegetation supporting plenty of game (2). White Lodge hill at over 40m, overlooking the Beverley Brook has yielded both Palaeolithic and Mesolithic flints. (location 1) A considerable quantity of Mesolithic stone tools has been found at a number of locations including Dann's Pond near Ladderstile gate and Ham Dip pond near Ham gate (6). (location 4)

In 1958 L.W. Carpenter, an experienced archaeologist, presented his view that underneath the top layer of gravel and sand on much of the higher ground in Richmond Park there was a high probability that other sites would be discovered. He was also of the opinion that comparatively undisturbed sites lie underneath the Petersham and Ham Common land (which were enclosed into the Park in 1637) as they have not been subjected to significant cultivation (7).

Lacaille similarly believed that a thorough investigation of the higher ground of Richmond Park would disclose material of great archaeological importance (2).

Research is now heavily reliant on the accounts of these early collectors of artefacts from Ham because the terrain within modern Ham has since changed beyond all recognition. Extensive gravel workings near Coldharbour throughout the first half of the 20th century created huge pits. Following the First World War much of the land of Ham Fields was progressively used to build houses. Furthermore, much of the remaining open area of Ham lands has been contaminated by thousands of tonnes of bomb debris brought from other parts of London to fill in the gravel pits and level the land. Any new findings in Ham Fields would therefore be of doubtful origin.

Above: A Mesolithic mace head discovered at the Thames foreshore in Ham

Left: Flint adze from the Mesolithic era found near Coldharbour

An Island Race with Continuous Immigration

With a warming climate the huge sheets of ice began to melt, creating a rise in the sea level. Sometime after 8000 BC the last dry land bridge between Anglia and Holland (also known as Doggerland) was turned into marshland. Within a further 2000 years the marshes had also succumbed to the sea.

Britain was now an Island and a day visit to the Continent was a lot more difficult. Nevertheless it was people arriving by boat from the Continent

that continued to significantly influence both human development and their interaction with the surrounding environment.

Left: The narrow land bridge has now been covered by the sea, making Britain an Island

Below: A wild boar, a wolf and a wild horse of the Mesolithic Age

Reluctance to Change

The defined Mesolithic era lasted nearly three times as long as the Christian Calendar of 2000 years. Even at the end of this period the hunter-gatherers based at Ham were apparently reluctant to shake off their nomadic way of life!

Deferred Settlement

The Neolithic Period
4000 BC to 2,500 BC

A new era dawned, the Neolithic age, a period when structured farming with techniques and livestock, introduced from Europe, established a settled routine of life across the landscape.

Yet it is very likely that the accomplished nomadic hunter-gatherers based at Ham were not yet ready for a settled routine. The abundance of animals, waterfowl and fish, readily available all year round, and a fertile environment on the margins of the river, supporting edible plants, berries and nuts, deferred the need for structured farming. It is therefore more likely that at this stage simple herding would have been attempted with a limited try at arable cultivation. Established farming and the constraints of settled society were delayed for a little longer.

A Settlement in Ham?
(location 2)

Field in his study of the Edwards, Finny and Knowles collection of artefacts found in Ham fields near Coldharbour, concluded that there was evidence of considerable settlement in the area during the Neolithic period, though less habitation than during the Mesolithic period. The main evidence comes from ground axes and arrowheads. All of the complete axes discovered display evidence of heavy use and were most probably discarded because they were damaged. The number of ground axes used and the accompanying flakes tended to indicate a permanent rather than a nomadic existence (1).

> Neolithic (Greek)
> Neo - new
> Lithos - stone
> hence "new stone age"

The Need for Effective Tools

The riverbed at Ham was full of large nodules of flint, which were ideal for making sharp tools. At this time axes and knives were first roughed out by knapping and then polished using abrasive sand and water or an abrasive tool. Though more time consuming, the tool benefitted from a more durable cutting edge that could easily be sharpened rather than simply being discarded (2).

Above: Hunting remained a preferred way of life to farming!

Below: A Neolithic flint axe in pristine condition dated around 4000 BC was found in 1953 in the Isabella plantation. (location 6)

Clearing and Managing the Forests

Equipped with flint axes with a renewable cutting edge or more robust axes made out of polished stone, generations of people at the Ham base progressively cleared elm and oak woodland on the gravel terraces and scrub alder on the floodplain.

Felling trees with axes expended a lot of energy, so an alternative practice evolved of killing trees by ring barking. Once dead, the trees were either left to collapse or were pulled over and burnt. Grass now had the opportunity to grow in the sunlight and this provided grazing for domesticated animals.

Continuous grazing, in turn, prevented the regrowth of shoots of trees. Some of this land could also be used for the growing of cereals (3).

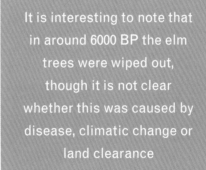

It is interesting to note that in around 6000 BP the elm trees were wiped out, though it is not clear whether this was caused by disease, climatic change or land clearance

Construction of Houses

The Thames provided a wide range of natural resources such as reeds, rushes and timber for building. There is, however, no evidence of any Neolithic houses in the location of Coldharbour or Ham fields. But this might be because:

- The gravel pits were excavated so quickly with scant regard to the historical treasure trove that lay amidst them, that any evidence has simply been lost.

- The evidence of these early settlements is yet to be found.

- The people continued to live in their traditional nomadic shelters.

Tree felling in the Neolithic period

Hunting

As hunting remained such a focal point of their lives, the people at the Coldharbour base would have continuously refined their hunting weapons to improve their success rate when hunting red and roe deer, wild boar and aurochs (the wild ox of the time). Arrow shafts needed to be cut and fletched and fixed securely to more effective flint tips. Strips of hide served as the means of securely attaching axes, spear and arrowheads to the shafts.

It is also likely that disputes over land and resources increasingly led to inter group battles and effective weapons would have been shaped with this in mind (4).

One of ten Leaf shaped arrowheads found at Walkers Market Garden, now Parkleys

Below left: An Aurochs skull. The original wild ox of Britain reached a height of nearly 2 metres

Knowles collected 49 arrowheads from Ham, half of them leaf shaped. These may have been used for both hunting and territorial disputes (1). Ten leaf shaped Neolithic arrow heads were found at Walkers Farm, now the location of Parkleys indicating that this was a popular location for hunting (1). (location 7). Flint debris has also been found in the location of Tudor Drive.

Food – Trial & Error

In the vicinity of Ham, wildlife continued to be plentiful. As well as fresh water, the Thames provided an abundant supply of fish, eels, birds, and small animals such as beavers and otters. Bird life included wild duck, goose and swan.

Seasonal runs of salmon and eels and migrating birds would have added to the feast. This all continued to make the Thames valley and the settlement at Ham a very comfortable place to live (1).

Many herbs were present in the woods and long established trial and error would have proved which plants and roots were edible and which were not! The diet was supplemented with woodland fruit and nuts including blackberries, sloes, wild cherries, hazel and beech nuts (3).

Top: A sheep of the Neolithic and below, a goat of the same period

Later in the period wheat, corn and barley were cultivated. The women and children would have learned to grind the cereal and bake coarse bread and cakes. Cereals were also used to make porridge and beer (3).

From the sheep and goats that were introduced from the Continent, milk and cheese became available.

Developing the Art of Cooking

Cookery was very much a developing art with plenty of trial and probably a fair amount of error! Yet the nutrition provided by the food had to more than compensate for the energy employed in making it.

Making Pots

The Neolithic era was also generally defined by the making of pottery. Surprisingly, no Neolithic period pottery was recovered from the Coldharbour site though again it may simply be that the settlement areas were so quickly excavated for gravel in the early 20th Century that there was no opportunity to capture the evidence.

Or was the making of pottery, just like serious farming, simply deferred by the inhabitants of Ham to a later age?

The discovery of pottery immediately implies settlement. Pottery requires the careful control of high temperature, not something that a nomadic hunting tribe would have much patience for.

Legacy

By now "Old Father Thames" seems to have taken on a spiritual significance and ritual offerings to this sacred stream included pots, bone and antler tools as well as flint and stone axes (5). The axes found in the river were invariably in good condition, in contrast to land sites where axes were often damaged (6).

At least nine stone and flint axes have been found in the river between the Ham and Twickenham banks and some had been exchanged over a very great distance. An axe made of greenstone/epidiorite found upstream of Eel Pie island probably came from Devon or Cornwall while a tuff axe has been linked to an axe factory at Pike O'Stickle in the Lake District (6).

These highly polished axes, especially those made of rare stone may also have been considered as an early symbol of power and authority (5).

Yet the Nomadic way of life provided little opportunity to build any reserves or surplus with which to exchange. The increasing need to acquire symbols of power and authority or votive offerings may have now served as a stimulus to adapt to a more settled way of life to provide the surplus with which to exchange.

The Construction of Barrows during the Neolithic Period

To leave a permanent record of their existence on the land, many of the people in the Neolithic period began building long barrows to provide final resting places for their dead.

Typically a barrow would have been a mound of earth, 30-40 m long with one end being taller and wider. Barrows would have been situated a healthy distance away from homesteads, usually on the summit of a hill or a ridge.

The barrow represented the earthly house of the deceased. The relics left inside were intended to be of use to the deceased in the after world. These objects were ritually broken to allow the spirit in them to be freed. Feasting was a prominent feature at the burial of a chieftain. In many cases flakes and worked flints have been found scattered in the mound (7). The modern practice of scattering flowers in and on the grave has been attributed to the pagan practice of scattering flint on the mounds.

Neolithic Monuments in the Parish of Ham
(location 9)

In 1630 Elias Allen produced a map of Richmond Park. North east of Ham Gate he marked a mound with a large tree on top (8).

Edward Jesse in 1835 noted that there were in this area;
"two or three ancient British Barrows... in which some broken pottery and deposits of ashes have been found. Immediately adjoining them, one of the finest oak-trees in the park may be seen." (9).

Left: Elias Allen Map of 1630 showing a large tree on a raised mound near Ham Gate

In 1843 Ede published a map of Richmond Park in which he identifies a barrow north east of Ham Gate.

Beighton writing in "The Leisure Hour" in 1887 recorded;
"Keeping on the footpath… we come to the round seat encircling one of the grandest oaks of the park, and opposite to it is a steep mound, in which have been found ancient weapons of war." (10).

In May 1990 Dr. Tom Greeves, a cultural environmentalist, was commissioned by the Royal Parks to carry out archaeological field research on an area of ground in the west of Richmond Park close to

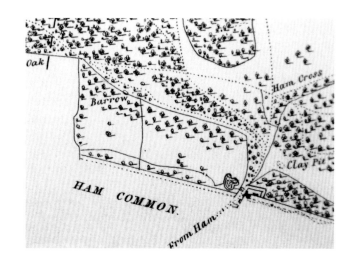

Left: Ede's 1843 map of Richmond Park clearly shows a barrow north east of Ham Gate

Ham Gate. Dr. Greeves meticulously explored the landscape looking for evidence of the ancient people who had lived and worked in the area (11). He was invited back in 1992 to carry out a full examination of the entire park (12).

Dr. Greeves' investigation disclosed what he considered to be a site of major importance (a long barrow) located on the ridge, north east of Ham Gate. Both its north and south ends appear to have been re-modelled at some time to create level platforms. He concluded that this; *"is almost certainly a well preserved long barrow, 40m long x 23m wide and still standing to a height of 2-3m."*

"About 20m north of the long barrow is an ancient oak tree set within an apparent prehistoric ring bank, 10m in diameter. The oak tree was well known as John Martin's oak."

(John Martin was a romantic painter, 1789-1854, who featured the tree in one of his paintings).

"On the east side of the long barrow are three shallow circular pits, each approx. 4m diameter x 0.5m deep. These may be prehistoric pits with a funerary/ritual function."

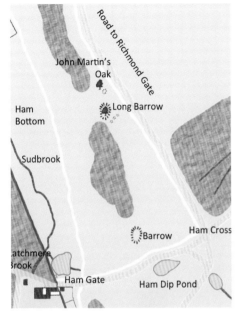

*The view from the top of the Terrace with the sun setting over the distant Surrey hills.
A good place for a burial mound?*

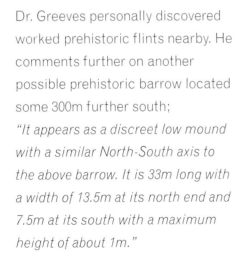

Dr. Greeves personally discovered worked prehistoric flints nearby. He comments further on another possible prehistoric barrow located some 300m further south;
"It appears as a discreet low mound with a similar North-South axis to the above barrow. It is 33m long with a width of 13.5m at its north end and 7.5m at its south with a maximum height of about 1m."

Prehistoric flints have been found on the east side of the mound and a Neolithic polished flint axe was found in the vicinity of Ham Gate (13). (location 8)

There was undoubtedly a lot of activity during the Neolithic period in Ham and the land contained within Richmond Park. Yet the Neolithic people in Ham seemed a little slow in taking up the practices and rituals normally associated with Neolithic folk in the rest of the country. Could it be that they identified natural mounds within the landscape and adapted them to serve as barrows or were these barrows created during the subsequent Bronze Age?

Dr. Greeves appropriately concludes his studies of the area within the Park;
"It is quite clear that there was prehistoric activity within the Park, perhaps stretching over several thousand years.

This is an historic landscape of major national significance, mainly because of the fact that the archaeological features though very subtle have survived so close to Central London."

Metal Divides

The Bronze Age 2,100 BC to 700 BC

Although the ability to produce gold and copper existed in Britain as early as 2,500 BC, bronze was not introduced until around 2,100 BC. The addition of approximately 10% of tin to 90% of copper under high temperatures created a new metal known as Bronze that made tools and weapons, which maintained a sharper edge for a longer period of time. Over the next 1000 years the production of bronze was increasingly refined and the knowledge of its production requiring small furnaces and specialised bellows carefully guarded by the few. The emergence of bronze weapons and tools helped create a hierarchical society with power and wealth in the hands of a limited number of territorial leaders.

Proof of Settlement in Ham
(location 2)

Bronze age activity in Ham and clear evidence of settlement is indicated by the discovery near the Coldharbour settlement of an intact beaker. These bell-shaped earthenware vessels decorated with cords or combs may also have been placed in graves at the feet of the deceased (2).

Early Bronze Age beaker pottery found in Coldharbour (2,100 to 1,500 BC)

Bronze Age spear found in the Thames near Ham

A Changing Environment for the Settlers in Ham

With more effective tools, the semi-nomadic lifestyle gradually gave way to a more permanent settlement and an established way of life. Successive generations would have cleared more and more woodland on the drier ground of the higher gravel terraces to create an increasing patchwork of fields for growing cereals. However, this clearance of the woodland on the surrounding uplands resulted in soil erosion and seasonal flooding of the floodplain, which in turn created more fertile meadowland for grazing adjacent to the river.

With a small number of permanent fields requiring year-round attention, the Coldharbour farmstead is likely to have comprised of a few thatched round houses, occupied by members of an extended family. The farmstead may have been divided into an inner domestic area and an outer compound for livestock (2).

Over time, as an increasing population required a greater yield from the land, there would have been an increased focus on working the more productive soils and disregarding the poorer quality land. It was during the latter part of the Bronze Age that farming would have been undertaken seriously at Coldharbour with more ordered field systems and clearly defined land boundaries such as ditches or fences (3).

Herding and Hunting

At the Coldharbour settlement it is likely that cattle, sheep and goats provided a source of meat, milk and cheese as well as leather and wool. Domestic pigs may have been bred from the wild boar, which roamed the forests.

Domesticated dogs were similarly bred from indigenous wolves and trained for hunting, the herding of domestic animals and protection. During the late Bronze Age the spinning and weaving of wool became a routine activity within each farmstead and oxen were harnessed to an early form of plough known as an ard, to break up the heavy clay.

Barbed and tanged arrowheads were found in a number of locations in Ham (4). Red Deer and aurochs (the fierce ancestor of domestic cattle) continued to be hunted in wooded areas. The barbed and tanged arrowhead had now replaced the leaf shaped arrowhead as a more effective hunting tool because the arrowhead was less likely to be dislodged by an animal in flight. When used against humans the removal of the barb would cause significant trauma.

Barbed and tanged arrowheads dated from 2,500 BC to 1,500 BC found in Walker's Market Garden, now Parkleys. (location 7)

The barbs were to prevent the arrow loosening when the animal bolted

Bronze Workshops Established just South of Ham
(location 13)

In a study titled "Evidence for Bronze Age settlement of Coombe Warren, Kingston Hill", David Field and Stuart Needham suggest that the concentrations of the Bronze metalwork found in the West London stretch of the Thames reflect long term activity on the banks and imply local distributive and manufacturing centres (5).

Pure copper that was produced in a simple bowl-shaped furnace and supports evidence of bronze working in Kingston Hill

They further comment;
"It is tempting to suggest that the Kingston Hill settlement might represent one of the workshops supplying much of this material..."
"It seems likely that the later Bronze Age site extended a considerable distance to the north of the A308 perhaps as far as Richmond Park"

International Exchange

The production of Bronze, though controlled locally, still required the sourcing of copper and tin from distant locations and a surplus of grain, hides and textiles had to be generated within the community including Coldharbour to make this exchange. The manufactured Bronze itself was then exchanged for more exotic weapons, goods, adornments and ornaments which were available on the Continent (3). The Thames provided the natural link between communities on its banks and the Continental and Irish ports and as a result the settlements along the Thames evolved as important trading bases.

Their leaders who closely managed both the production of the Bronze and the onward trade, grew increasingly wealthy and with wealth came power, prestige and patronage (1).

Supporting an Elite Ruling Class

These increasingly powerful leaders reinforced their position through sponsorship of a loyal band of warriors and skilled metal smiths. Feasting and the gifting of weapons, tools, adornments and ornaments helped to further emphasise their authority (2).

The gains from raids on neighbouring communities and the extortion of a protection tax from farmsteads under the rule of the leader will have provided the means to support a fortified settlement and the growing aspirations of the leader, his extended family and his warriors.

Any remaining surplus could be used as exchange for more refined clothing, adornments, ornaments, weapons and armour that gave the leader, his family and the warriors more prestige and clearly identified their status within the community.

Border Disputes

With increasing competition for resources, the borders of such territories were likely to have been in continuous dispute. As a result the farming routine of the extended family at Coldharbour was likely to have been regularly disrupted by raids from bordering warrior groups, either to seize cattle or with demands for allegiance with payment for commensurate protection (6).

The warrior aristocracy now cultivated an elite lifestyle of feasting and fighting that was to set a trend for subsequent generations of warriors in Britain. The horse, a descendant of the Paleolithic

wild horse that ranged throughout Britain in earlier times, was broken in and trained for warfare. The use of metal weapons and a progressive ability to fight on horseback will have transformed combat. A leader could now have a small band of mounted warriors who could quickly respond to any local skirmish or carry out a raid for cattle in a rival territory (6).

This bronze sword has an expanded leaf-shaped blade and was found in the Thames at Richmond. Warriors used these weapons in a downward slashing motion, possibly while on horseback. This is very similar to the sword found in the Thames opposite Pope's Villa (location 11)

Aubrey's Ramp – A Bronze Age Construction?
(location 10)

To avoid any doubt as to the limits of their territory and reinforce their authority, Community leaders needed to establish clearly defined ditched boundaries. Some of the linear ditches may also have been intended to control access to springs in lowland areas where long linear earthworks cut off bends in the Thames (3).

Climate change was also having a serious impact on the local environment. A rising sea level would have caused the tidal head to move further up the Thames Valley resulting in more regular flooding of

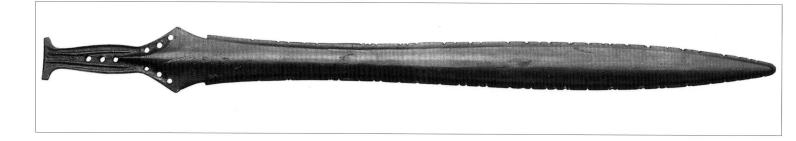

...in Ham-heath runs a straight Rampire from the Parke towards Thames, having the graffe westwards: it is likely this way made as an obstacle to the Romans;

riverside grazing land and woodland. To maintain access to traditional hunting and rich grazing land beside the river, people were forced to construct elevated trackways (2).

The earliest record of a possible prehistoric ditched earthwork in the area of Ham was made by John Aubrey in the late 1600s. Aubrey was a pioneer archaeologist, who recorded, often for the first time, numerous megalithic and other field monuments in the south of England. He also referred to an earthwork on Whitmoor Common, Worplesdon that has proved to be a Bronze Age track cutting through a coaxial field system.

In his Monumenta Britannica (7) he noted:
"...in Ham heath runs a straight Rampire from the Parke towards Thames having the graffe (ditch) westwards, it is likely that this was made as an obstacle to the Romans."

In 1726, not too long after Aubrey published his Monumenta Britannica, there was an interesting dispute between the 3rd Earl of Dysart, Lord of the Manor of Ham and a Mr. Hardinge, Lord of the Manor of Canbury located between Kingston and Ham. The dispute arose from the keeping of hogs and general encroachment by the Lord of the Manor of Canbury on Ham Common which was contested by the Lord and people of Ham. The

issue of a clearly defined border arose and reference was made to a ditch known as the Party ditch that ran through a great part of Ham Common;
"...it was the Boundary of extent of Hatch (a sub hamlet of Ham) tho (Lord of the Manor of Ham) can give no account why that Ditch was made tho it is yet visible it may well be presumed to be a boundary ditch... and so reputed and made for that purpose."

This ditch was referred to as early as 1615 as a location reference in a case against a man for cutting down a tree. So well before the creation of Richmond Park we have evidence of a clearly defined boundary.

Was this the same ditch (graffe) noted by John Aubrey and was it an ancient ditch as Aubrey alludes?

Top: Aubrey's hand written account of the Rampire running through Ham heath

Right: A raised ramp running left to right at the top of the picture seen from the flooded woods

An Ancient Path in Ham still used today?

A straight line drawn from the Upper terraces in Richmond Park along the elevated path shown below arrives at the River Thames near to the Coldharbour settlement, near a clearly defined bend in the river.

Unanswered Questions

- Was a rampire formed in the Bronze Age, when ditches were dug to both define and drain plots of land?

- Or in the form of a linear earthwork, was it a territorial boundary that stretched for miles as far as the river?

- Did it, at a later time, become a convenient practical walkway allowing continuous easy access to Coldharbour for both men and cattle during the wetter winter months when the river flooded the adjacent plains?

Was this "Coldharbour Lane", the first road in Ham providing access to the river?

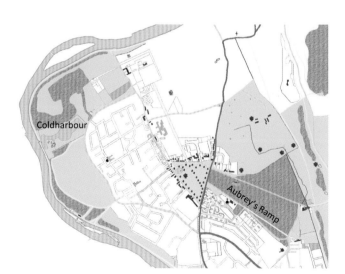

Coldharbour

Aubrey's Ramp

Left: Map showing the direction of Aubrey's ramp in relation to the Coldharbour settlement

Top right: Funerary Rites on the bank of the Thames

Ritual and Burial

Ritual now came to dominate all aspects of life and it is likely that at the Coldharbour settlement the house entrances were aligned with the rising sun (2). For the Community in the vicinity of Ham, the Thames itself was the dominant natural feature of the landscape.

Unlike the large ceremonial monuments of the Neolithic period, which required a lot of manpower, burial of the dead with less pomp would have been carried out close to the Coldharbour settlement. The dead were cremated and their ashes, contained in small pots, were placed in small urnfields (2).

Lidar survey showing the continuation of the linear feature through Ham Common

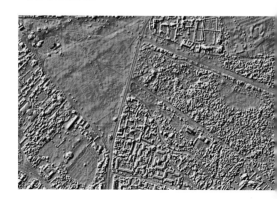

A Bronze Age Urnfield near Coldharbour?
(location 2)

Knowles, one of the more prolific collectors of artefacts in the area, recovered three collared urns, one of which bears the fingernail marks of its maker. Knowles also noted the presence of many urns, being found near the *"Red Barn of Coldharbour,"* which tended to break up when touched (4).

Bob Cowie in an article on Prehistoric Twickenham referred extensively to Ham Fields and concluded:
"The possibility that there may have been prehistoric burial sites in Ham Fields should be seriously considered especially as two riverside burial mound sites have been recorded in Teddington and Hurst Park in East Molesey."

Votive Offerings

From about 3,500 BP, bronze spears, swords and other weapons were deposited in the river in large numbers between Kingston and London Bridge with particularly large concentrations of finds immediately downstream from Ham at Richmond and Syon Reach (9). Such weapons would have been deposited by the new elite and the warrior class, not the poorer farmers of Coldharbour and neighbouring settlements. Perhaps this elite class were based at a settlement near Kingston Hill but they selected the Thames downriver from Ham as a favoured spot to make their ritual offerings.

Many of the weapons since discovered were damaged with tips of spears broken off and swords broken in half. The deliberate act of putting a weapon out of commission with no chance of recovery indicates that the items have been surrendered to the river to pass on to another world.

Some weapons may also have been lost by accident or during skirmishes, providing evidence of increasing social tension. Other weapons have been eroded from riverbank sites such as Syon Park where a later Bronze Age hoard was exposed by erosion (10).

Just north of the Coldharbour settlement opposite Pope's Villa in Teddington, a bronze sword was found in the river Thames, some 20 yards from the Middlesex bank. The edges of the sword had been deliberately damaged rendering it no longer serviceable. (location 11)

Stoney Jack

George Fabian Lawrence (1861 – 1939), known as Stoney Jack was the son of a pawnbroker with a wider ambition. His most notable claim to fame was as the man who brought to light the Cheapside Hoard, a treasure trove of more than 400 pieces of Elizabethan and Jacobean jewellery and ornaments, discovered in 1912 by workmen using a pickaxe to excavate in a cellar at Cheapside in London.

He put word out among the mudlarks who searched the Thames foreshore at low tide and the navvies who dug the foundations of buildings in London that he would pay cash and ask few questions if they presented him with items of interest. For the newly founded London Museum, he was employed as "Inspector of Excavations" and during this period he contributed significantly to their collections (11).

In "Antiquities from the Middle Thames" written in 1929 Lawrence details many of the findings in the river Thames in the vicinity of Ham (12).

Near the "one tree" (now known as the Half Mile Tree, where Lower Ham Road joins the river): (location 12)

- a short bronze dirk
- a bronze spear butt worn at the side
- a bronze chisel and a bronze drill

Opposite Pope's Villa (location 11)

- two dagger blades
- a spearhead
- two axes
- a leaf shaped sword
- a flint dagger

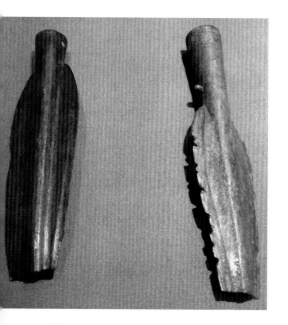

Left: Damaged Bronze Age spearheads found in the Thames near Ham

Right: George Fabian Lawrence (1861 – 1939) known as Stoney Jack

Metal Divides

The social elite of the diverse communities in the Thames Valley, through production of metal, marriage and exchange had by the Late Bronze Age formed strong alliances with equivalent status groups in both Ireland and the Continent (3). Despite increasing competition for resources, resolved by regular conflict, this was a period of growing prosperity for them.

Left: Bronze Dirk found in the Thames near Half Mile Tree

Below: Bronze Spear Butt found in the Thames in the area of Ham

Around 800 BC the supply of copper, necessary for the production of bronze, apparently dried up and the established exchange system and social hierarchy was put under great pressure. Those who were able to adapt quickest and use their alliances to best effect to provide new metal making techniques, military skills and a continuing source of metal were destined to survive and flourish (3).

Meanwhile the farmers at Coldharbour and other settlements in the Thames Valley continued to follow the rhythm of the seasons, cultivating their crops and tending their cattle. Coldharbour was located with one known river border immediately to the north and perhaps another ditched land border directly to the east.
The settlers here would have paid taxes and protection money, though probably received little protection. It is likely that they lived in perpetual fear of rapid territorial raids from across the borders. Ultimately they would have had to manage their own meagre defence with cruder weapons and perhaps the breeding of large dogs which would have given them early warning and served as something of a deterrent!

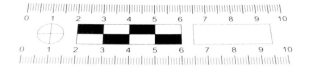

The Influence of Rome

The Iron Age
700 BC to AD 43

An increasing shortage in the supply of copper and tin exacerbated by the intensifying demands of the burgeoning Roman Empire led to the emergence of the Age of Iron. Difficulties began in about 1,100 BC and became especially severe during the ninth century BC. The introduction of ironworking to the lower Thames Valley in around 650 BC was to prove one of the most defining changes of the period (1).

Iron, made from a more widely available ore, improved the productivity of the smaller settlements by providing them with the opportunity to directly produce stronger metal tools and weapons (2). Over time this gradually weakened the stranglehold that the Bronze Age Elite had exerted over the farming settlements through their control over the production and distribution of bronze weapons, tools and the trade of valued accoutrements (3).

But now the Elite had to quickly adapt to changing circumstances to survive. They would also need to establish alliances with the powerful elite in Rome alongside their traditional alliances in Gaul and Ireland.

As the Age neared its finale, a Roman Tempest headed by Julius Caesar was destined to scythe its way through North East Surrey and undoubtedly leave a profound impression on the people who were settled there.

Sherd from a barrel

Evidence of an Iron Age Settlement in Ham
(location 16)

Several pieces of pottery, some near-complete vessels, were found by Edwards at the Coldharbour site. The following items are considered to be from the late Iron Age period (4).

- Two sherds of pottery from the same vessel decorated with grooved horizontal bands. The decoration is similar to pottery found at an Iron Age/ Romano-British settlement at Old Malden. A model of the Old Malden settlement is shown in Kingston Museum. This model gives us a good idea of the nature of the settlement in Ham at Coldharbour.

- Two carinated jars with moulded collars considered to be late Iron Age and a sherd from a barrel beaker decorated with vertical grooved arcs positioned between two grooved horizontal bands.

- Three other carinated jars with their base missing indicating that they were buried upside down and the base was smashed during ploughing. Such vessels were associated with burials. Unfortunately, two thousand years of annual ploughing in Ham fields is likely to have scattered and destroyed much of the evidence from this earlier period.

- Fragments from Iron Age quernstones were also found at the site.

- Among the Knowles collection of artifacts found in Ham were 36 pieces of a late Iron Age bowl. These were located in the sand about 200 yards from the river, not far from the red roofed barn (Coldharbour) (4).

Three thousand years ago, the temperature fell by as much as two degrees centigrade and the climate in southern England became progressively damper. Though a relatively small change in temperature, this meant that the growing season was dramatically shortened, by up to 5 weeks (7).

With an increasing population, the land continued to be steadily stripped of forests and turned to the plough. This deforestation resulted in much fertile soil being washed by the rains into the Thames. A growing population with an increasing demand for food, both for consumption and trade, now put greater stress on food production. It became imperative to find more efficient ways to maximise the output of food throughout the land (7).

Sometime after 100 BC coins were produced in Britain from tin rich bronze known as potin. They were probably used for direct transactions at markets at community boundaries. A small hoard of nine tin coins has been found on Eel Pie Island (5). (location 17)

Several pieces of Iron Age and Roman pottery dating from the 1st century BC were discovered near a riding ring just north of Bog Lodge in Richmond Park (6).

With such evidence of settlement, especially during the latter part of the Age, it is helpful to pause and consider the changing nature of the environment, the daily routine of the people and the key influences on their life.

Top: Model of an Iron Age settlement shown in the Kingston Museum

Left: Iron Age coin from a hoard of potin coins found at Eel Pie Island

Above: Iron Age Homestead

The People

During the Iron Age the floodplain of the Thames was settled by small farmsteads, such as Coldharbour, to make efficient use of the rich summer grazing. It is likely that the Coldharbour settlement supported an extended family and their livestock during the warmer months.

They would probably have moved to a homestead on higher ground during the winter when the land by the river was prone to flooding. Over the years, an expanding clan is likely to have emerged, each family unit with their own defined farmstead competing to maximise the resources of the land and the river.

The Coldharbour Farmstead

People at this time typically lived in round houses with densely thatched roofs. Wattle walls were made from a framework of upright timbers interwoven with coppiced hazel or willow poles. This was then covered with a daub made from clay, straw and animal dung that effectively weatherproofed the house and helped retain the warmth.

Within the farmstead were pens for the animals, large sealed pits used for storing grain for planting, and small granaries raised above the ground on posts to keep the grain for consumption away from rodents [9].

At the centre of the house was an open-hearth fire, which would have been maintained at all times. A bronze cauldron might be suspended from a tripod, by a chain, over the fire.

Left: The Iron Age witnessed more intensive working of the land to increase food production

Right: Looms enabled more effective production of brightly coloured material

Governed by the Seasons and the Daily Routine of the Farmstead

The people of the Coldharbour settlement followed a daily routine interrupted only by the religious festivals that marked the changing of the seasons.

On the more fertile riverside land it is reasonable to assume that a variety of animals including cattle, sheep, goats and pigs were managed for food, fuel and hides.

Most farmers also grew a mixture of wheat, barley, rye and oats.

Towards the end of the Age the domestic cat and the Indian jungle fowl that we now know as chicken were introduced into Britain. Horses were harnessed for pulling four wheeled carts and dogs continued to assist in the herding of livestock and hunting (9).

The introduction of an iron tip to the wooden plough, known as an ard, gave farmers the ability to gouge the richer but heavier soil of the valley floor (10).

Iron sickles were used for cutting and shaping branches and wood. Trees needed to be carefully managed to ensure an adequate supply of timber to make buildings, tools and vehicles, and also provide sufficient firewood and charcoal. Farmers also spent time laying and maintaining miles of hedges to define the boundaries of the fields and settlements.

In contrast to the days of ease of the Mesolithic hunter-gatherers, the people at Coldharbour during the Iron Age would have found their time increasingly occupied. Aside from the daily maintenance of the farmstead, the crops and the livestock, numerous domestic chores had to be attended to. The introduction of the potters wheel from the Continent enabled the people to make more regular shaped beakers, cups, dishes and flagons. Other utensils could be shaped from wood. Looms, using clay weights, enabled them to make large pieces of brightly coloured and patterned cloth, which in turn was used to make clothing and blankets. Some settlements specialised in making iron, salt, or quern stones which they traded for other commodities (10). Generating a surplus on the farmstead provided the community with the means of trading for more specialist metals, ornaments and other luxuries found on the Continent.

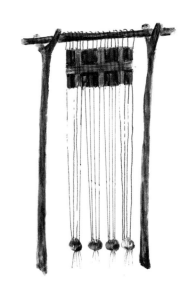

A Revolutionary Domestic Appliance

Iron Age rotatory querns made flour-making much quicker and easier than the traditional saddle querns. This was an important new technology that probably transformed daily life in Iron Age Britain. Quern stones, from this period found at Coldharbour, were used to grind grains of wheat, barley or rye into flour to make bread and other foods.

Food

The flour from wheat and barley was used to make bread. Grain was fermented to make beer and the surface foam was scraped off to make a lighter kind of bread. Barley and rye may have been used to make porridge.

Milk and dairy products were readily available from the cattle and the river at Coldharbour

A rotatory quern consisted of two quern stones, the top stone being rotated above the fixed lower stone. The hard abrasive surfaces of the quern stones moving against each other ground grains into flour (10)

continued to provide an abundance of fish and waterfowl. The diet of the settlement, could also be supplemented with edible berries, nuts, flowers and roots with the addition of honey to sweeten food.

The smoky interior of the house was ideal for the drying and preservation of meat, fish and herbs. Salt was also used for preserving meat (9).

Worship

The people did not worship in temples but on the farm and in the countryside and made offerings to various gods, spirits and ancestors. Weapons continued to be offered in rivers by the elite, and common tools such as pots, querns and utensils were offered at simpler farmsteads (10).

Festivals relating to the passage of the seasons and the management of the crops were now clearly an essential part of the annual calendar and had superseded in importance the summer and winter solstice.

The predominant method of disposing of the dead continued to be cremation, with the ashes being buried in urns. By the fifth century BC, the dearth of evidence of burials tends to indicate that cremated remains were scattered, or committed to the river. Alternatively, bodies may simply have been left in the open for animals and crows to scavenge!

A Hierarchical Society Evolves

As the Iron Age evolved, society in southern Britain became increasingly hierarchical. At the lowest level were captured slaves to work on the land. Above them were the tenant farmers who were permanently in debt to the community leader. At the top of the social pyramid were the elite class consisting of the extended family of the leader, a loyal band of warriors and the learned class consisting of druids, bards and seers (3).

The Druids

During the Iron Age, the Druids acted as intermediaries between the people and the Gods and were in charge of all rituals and sacrifices. Within society they were equal to the highest of the warrior class but to attain this, initiates had to endure 20 years of study (without the use of pen and paper to facilitate their learning). They were involved in the settling of disputes between individuals and communities and anyone who failed to abide by their rule was ostracised from society. The Druids believed that after death the soul passed from one body to another. This helped to remove the fear of death and supposedly made the warriors braver, albeit more reckless in battle, something noted by Julius Caesar (7).

Power bases in Southern England

With cultivation of the land being maximised, powerful leaders looked to expand their territories and with the support of kin groups in Gaul, engaged in raids and open warfare on neighbouring territories (3).

In this way the smaller territories of the Bronze age coalesced into larger Kingdoms headed by an aristocratic class and centred

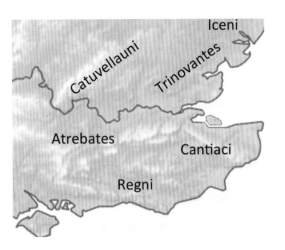

Map showing the location of the rival communities

further inland away from the Thames. The Atrebates gradually came to control an area of land now known as Hampshire, West Sussex, Berkshire and Surrey. The Catuvellauni, a powerful and combative group, based in present day Hertfordshire, meanwhile expanded their dominion south to the Middlesex bank of the Thames. Only the kingdoms with the most capable and ruthless leaders supported by a skilled fighting warrior corps survived.

The Thames became a clearly defined border between the two groups and the fertile settlement at Coldharbour would have been very visible to warriors from rival communities!

Hill Forts

It became something of a fashion within the Iron Age for territorial leaders to construct hill forts. Located on high ground, they were surrounded by earth banks and ditches to serve as a place of retreat when under attack. They also served as a visible monument that projected the power of the leader. After all, the huge amount of effort and resources required to build such a fort required the collective energy of the community and this could only be demanded by a powerful leader (7).

In around 700 BC a defended hill top settlement was established on Wimbledon Common with a single

bank and a 12 feet deep, 30 feet wide ditch enclosing an area of about 12 acres. Evidence of post holes also suggests a timber palisade and revetment (11). It is confusingly nowadays identified as Cæsar's camp (location 15).

This may have provided a secure location for the leader, his family and his warriors, a storehouse and armoury and specialist workmen who could make both weapons and tools. The leader assigned the right to work a piece of land and with it a degree of protection in return for a percentage of the crops, hides or wool. In return for the loyalty of the tax paying subjects, the leader allowed them to farm undisturbed. Without payment of the tax they would have been under threat of being evicted from the land (3).

In his 1992 survey of Richmond Park, Dr. Tom Greeves identified a possible Hill Fort on the north side of Broomfield Hill overlooking the

Satisfying the Needs of Rome

By 120 BC Rome had become the centre of a thriving trading market that extended to the farthest reaches of its expanding Empire. The voracious consumer society in Rome demanded an ever-increasing amount of raw materials, food, slaves and mercenary soldiers to sustain its growth (13).

Strabo (a Greek geographer, philosopher and historian who lived between 64 BC to AD 24) commented on goods exported from Britain;
"It bears grain, cattle, gold, silver, and iron. These things, accordingly, are exported from the island, as also hides, and slaves, and dogs that are by nature suited to the purposes of the chase" (14).

An increasing need from the elite class within Southern Britain for Roman wine, ornaments and other accoutrements favoured by the elite in Rome was satisfied by the exchange of slaves, hunting dogs and other goods. Many of the British leaders may have sent their sons to be educated in Rome to extend their network of connections and alliances.

The Demand for Slaves

Raids into adjacent territories helped maintain a continuous flow of slaves and served as a means for young warriors to quickly achieve valuable experience, wealth and prestige. A considerable number of British men, women and children would have been captured and sold into slavery during this period.

As the powerful Kingdoms became progressively acquisitive and restless, the people living in the settlement at Ham would have increasingly had to look at defending themselves and safeguarding their valuable livestock.

the steepest and most tortuous section of road in Richmond Park. Today, cyclists will be only too familiar with the steep slope of this hill (12). (location 14).

Dr Greeves reported;
"On the north side of Broomfield Hill, the ground falls steeply and there are four (possibly five) concentric banks with ditches, which have the appearance of

Broomfield Hill, site of an Iron Age Hill Fort?

defensive earthworks. On the south west side of Broomfield Hill there are the remnants of a substantial double bank."

The defensive hill top settlement on Wimbledon Common is located only two kilometres away.

Fighting and warfare was now a way of life in Southern Britain and it was this readiness for warfare that enabled the British Communities to amass large numbers of competent warriors so quickly against each of the invading Roman armies. When Julius Caesar brought his legions to England in 55 BC and 54 BC he encountered a competent and battle hardened army of disparate Kingdoms led by the King of the Catuvellauni. The British warriors were not unfamiliar with the violence of war. Caesar, a veteran warrior himself, was surprised at how skillful the British warriors were in the use of horse drawn chariots, which had been introduced decades before.

Prestige through Conflict

Success in combat or a raid was a quick way for a young member of the warrior class to achieve a status among his peers. A successful warrior, through daring raids, could quickly amass wealth, followers and prestige. To young ambitious men this would have appeared far more desirable than spending years toiling in the field (7). Ideally, they would be revered as heroes, and their bravery and accomplishments would be sung about by the bards for many generations to come.

An unexpected night-time raid across the river to the Coldharbour settlement could easily have provided a valuable number of captives. The raiders would quickly exchange them on with a middleman for wine and weapons. Traded on to a Territorial leader near the coast, the unfortunate

prisoners would have been packed with other captives into a boat and transported overseas where they would have been sold as slaves to spend the rest of their lives in servitude (7).

In considering the location of the Coldharbour settlement sitting on an exposed frontier, the question could be asked, "how often did the inhabitants change with the ebb and flow of the relative strength of the rival Kingdoms?"

Above left: The Triumphs of Caesar – The Captives

Below: British tribes were accomplished in the use of the chariot in warfare

Even if the people of the settlement chose flight over fight, it is likely that the leaders of the Territory would still have demanded men from each of the settlements, under their assumed protection, to fight as foot soldiers in their battles. How much time did the settlers on the riverside at Ham and the high ground in Richmond Park allocate for training in the handling of the weapons of war either for defence or to take part in territorial battles?

Below: Feasting was the warrior ritual during which raids were briefed and raid members invited

The Weapons

From childhood, the men and women of the Iron Age would have spent time practising using a sling, a common and easily constructed weapon of the period that has its own biblical reputation (9). Easy to make from leather and hemp twine, this simple but lethal weapon had an effective, accurate range of about 60 metres. When released from the ramparts of a hill fort, sling-stones would provide a hail of effective fire on adversaries struggling up a slope.

The experienced warriors used spears and long slashing swords accompanied by shields of leather, sometimes overlaid with bronze. Many of the weapons that have survived from this era had a ceremonial purpose and were thrown into rivers. These ceremonial weapons tend to be more elaborate than the combat weapons used.

Top: Sling shot boys – the local gang of the Iron Age period!

Above: A sling shot most effectively used from the height of a hill fort

> **Oppidum- a settlement having walls and fortifications and serving as a provincial strong point.**

Warriors based in the fortified settlements drilled horses in pulling two wheeled chariots in preparation for battle.

Iron Age Oppidum in Putney

One unresolved question is why fine weapons and shields continued to be deposited in the Thames when the centres of the Kingdoms were believed to have moved so much further inland (3).

Discoveries of Gallic - Belgic coinage along with fine metal work and swords in the Thames, down river from Richmond, has given credence to the suggestion of a pre - Caesarian settlement (Oppidum) a few miles to the west of London which came to an end as a major site around 60 BC. Could this have been located at the existing tidal head of the Thames allowing trading vessels one tidal lift up from the sea? Numerous Thames-side finds of base "potin" coin, including the one at Eel Pie Island, imply the production and circulation of a localised currency that was terminated abruptly by some sort of emergency (15).

The Battersea Shield found in the Thames at Battersea Bridge

It has been suggested that this putative trading and political centre located somewhere near present day Putney might have grown instead of London if a sudden massive conflict had not arrested its development and the Thames been transformed from a major commercial trading route to a disputed frontier (15).

Caesar Invades Southern Britain

Julius Caesar carefully documented his campaigns in the South of Britain in 55 BC and 54 BC and recorded his observations in his commentary "The Gallic War' (16). This provides us with a fascinating insight into the nature and disposition of the British Kingdoms including the Atrebates and Catuvellauni. It also gives us an indication of the turmoil that is likely to have been inflicted on all settlements along the lower Thames Valley, including Coldharbour.

As a result of their geographical location in England and their close connections in Gaul, the Atrebates and Catuvellauni had become two of the most developed and prosperous rival kingdoms in Britain. At this time they were tentatively separated by the Thames River and their respective fortunes would come to depend much on the whim and success of Julius Caesar.

Caesar used the excuse that the Gauls had received assistance from the Britons during his campaigns in Gaul to invade Britain in 55 BC and 54 BC. This assistance, paid for in coin, issued by the Gallic Belgic Confederacy, was most likely in the supply of corn to replace devastated crops and warriors to make up losses inflicted by the Legions (15).

In August 55 BC, Caesar's Legions made an initial foray onto the southern coast of Britain but were denied the opportunity to venture into the interior by a combination of poor weather and the determined resistance of the British warriors united by Cassivellaunus, the King of the Catuvellauni. King Commius of the Atrebates, the ally of Caesar, had been unceremoniously secured in irons by the Britons throughout the limited campaign.

Roman soldiers confronting British warriors on British soil for the first time

Below: Roman infantry carrying heavy armour advancing

Just one year later Caesar returned to Britain commanding five legions, each of 5000 men and 2000 cavalry in over 800 ships. Without any resistance on the coast, Caesar's legions advanced steadily into southern Britain.

Although the Legions steadfastly fought their way through Kent and the north east corner of Surrey, Caesar was impressed by the tactics of the British warriors and their skillful use of chariots. (As many as 4000 were deployed against his Legions);

"... it was clear that the (Roman) infantry, owing to the weight of their armour, were ill fitted to engage an enemy of this kind; for they could not pursue him when he retreated, and they dared not abandon their regular formation: also that the cavalry

fought at great risk, because the enemy generally fell back on purpose, and, after drawing our men a little distance away from the legions, leaped down from their chariots and fought on foot with the odds in their favour... Besides, the Britons never fought in masses, but in groups separated by wide intervals; they posted reserves and relieved each other in succession, fresh vigorous men taking the places of those who were tired." (17).

Cassivellaunus resorted to guerilla warfare in an attempt to inhibit the progress of the Legions. Caesar's troops responded by ravaging the countryside, burning crops and torching villages (18).

In his pursuit of Cassivellaunus, Caesar had to cross the Thames somewhere west of present day London;

Having ascertained the enemy's plans, Caesar led his army to the Thames, into the territories of Cassivellaunus. The river can only be forded at one spot, and there with difficulty. On reaching this place, he observed that the enemy were drawn up in great force near the opposite bank of the river. The bank was fenced by sharp stakes planted along its edge; and similar stakes were fixed under water and concealed by the river. Having learned these facts from prisoners and deserters, Caesar sent his cavalry on in front, and ordered the legions to follow them speedily; but the men advanced with such swiftness and dash, though they only had their heads above water, that the enemy, unable to withstand the combined onset of infantry and cavalry, quitted the bank and fled (19).

One of the many considered Thames crossing points of Caesar and his legions is at Brentford. If this were the case, then Caesar would have assembled his vast force across the river on land,

which is now known as Kew Gardens, with the elite troops, wearing full armour, preparing to lead the crossing. It gives an added dimension to the journey past Kew Gardens on the top deck of a 65 bus.

It is also likely that mounted Roman scouts were advancing quickly along the south bank of the

Top: Roman troops crossing the Thames

Below: Roman scout passing through Ham seeking a suitable crossing point of the Thames and searching for forage for the legions

Thames past Coldharbour, looking for an ideal place to cross the river, reconnoitering the enemies' location and also identifying farms where they could get grain and meat to feed the legions. The scouts were probably aided by members of the Atrebates tribe keen to gain support from Caesar and regain territory that had been lost to the Catuvellauni.

Caesar pursued Cassivellaunus to his stronghold just north of modern day St Albans and despite the strength of its fortification, destroyed it. Many of the captured Britons were killed, though, Cassivellaunus managed to escape (20).

Caesar, needing to get his Legions back to Gaul to quell growing unrest, had no choice but to dispatch his loyal ally, King Commius of the Atrebates, to negotiate terms with Cassivellaunus.

Stability for Ham

With Caesar gone, never to return and King Commius of the Atrebates taking a sabbatical on the Continent, southern Britain was open to progressive subjugation by the Catuvellauni.

That is, unless the relationship with Rome and favourable terms offered to loyal Kingdoms to trade with the wider Roman economy provided a logical constraint to their territorial ambitions.

In this way the people of southern Britain would have been gradually absorbed into the trading market of the Roman Empire. An uneasy truce would have prevailed with the Thames serving as a clear boundary with the Catuvellauni to the north and the Atrebates to the south, though the political centres continued to be located well away from the Thames.

Caesar leaving Britain

Under these terms the people of Coldharbour are likely to have experienced a period of relative stability and peace.

The Pax Romana

AD 43 to AD 410

Evidence of Settlement in Ham during the Romano-British Period

During this period the Coldharbour settlement would have continued being used as a small farmstead. (location 16)

Pottery dating to the 1st or early 2nd Century, and an early Romano-British quernstone were found near Coldharbour in Ham Fields (1). Other finds included a decorated Roman vase, an urn and pieces of Roman glass bottles (3).

A cinerary urn of the early Roman period was "found alone", about a foot below the surface in blackened sand near the Ham Towpath just opposite the eastern point of Eel Pie Island (2). (location 18)

There is evidence of a Romano-British settlement including a possible temple on the slopes of Kingston/Coombe Hill on the border with Richmond Park and evidence of a Roman period settlement at Skerne Road in Kingston, just south of the border with Ham. There is also a burial ground of the period at Canbury Field (4).

Above: Roman cinerary urn

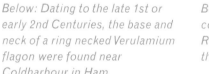

Below: Dating to the late 1st or early 2nd Centuries, the base and neck of a ring necked Verulamium flagon were found near Coldharbour in Ham

Below right: A complete example of a Roman flagon held in the Museum of London

Status Quo

Following the departure of Caesar, the economy of the southern part of England developed rapidly, with trading policies tactically favouring those tribes that deferred to Rome. The material luxuries and benefits of a wider Mediterranean economy became increasingly available to the submissive elite of Britain and slaves could now be bought and sold with currency (5).

The status quo was to be shattered on the death of King Cunobelin of the Catuvellauni in AD 42. His sons Caratacus and Togodumnus seized control of the Kingdom but could not resist a progressive encroachment into the territories of the neighbouring communities. They promptly declared war on the Atrebates, led by Verica. Coldharbour, a border settlement, could have been one of the first to suffer the predations of Catuvellauni warriors.

The Atrebates were routed, their capital captured and their lands seized. The deposed King Verica fled to Gaul and appealed for help from Rome. The territorial ambitions of the Catuvellauni and their blatant disregard of Rome finally served as a catalyst for the next Roman invasion, though, this time the Romans would stay a little longer!

General Aulus Plautius led four legions with 25,000 regular Roman soldiers with a comparable number of auxiliary soldiers. Yet again the British warriors led by the Catuvellauni relied on local knowledge of fords and currents and used rivers as lines of defence. But, just as before, this merely served as a temporary means of delaying the powerful Roman legions. The decisive battle was fought on the banks of the River Medway, close to Rochester.

Advancing Roman infantry encountering British Warriors

It has been suggested that the Iron Age Fort at Wimbledon Common was subsequently secured by the Legio II Augusta under Vespasian in their push westwards in AD 44 (6).

With the Romans indicating their intention to stay a little longer, the leaders of the Atrebates and other communities were more than willing to pledge their allegiance as client Kings in return for protection

and a level of influence and prestige within the newest satellite of the Roman Empire. Kingston and the surrounding area including Ham was likely to have fallen under the jurisdiction of the civitas of the Atrebates under the protection and patronage of their Roman rulers. Under such patronage, members of the Atrebates Tribe are likely to have moved quickly to secure possession of the Coldharbour and other riverside settlements.

At this stage, Prehistory in England came to a close and recorded history begins.

61

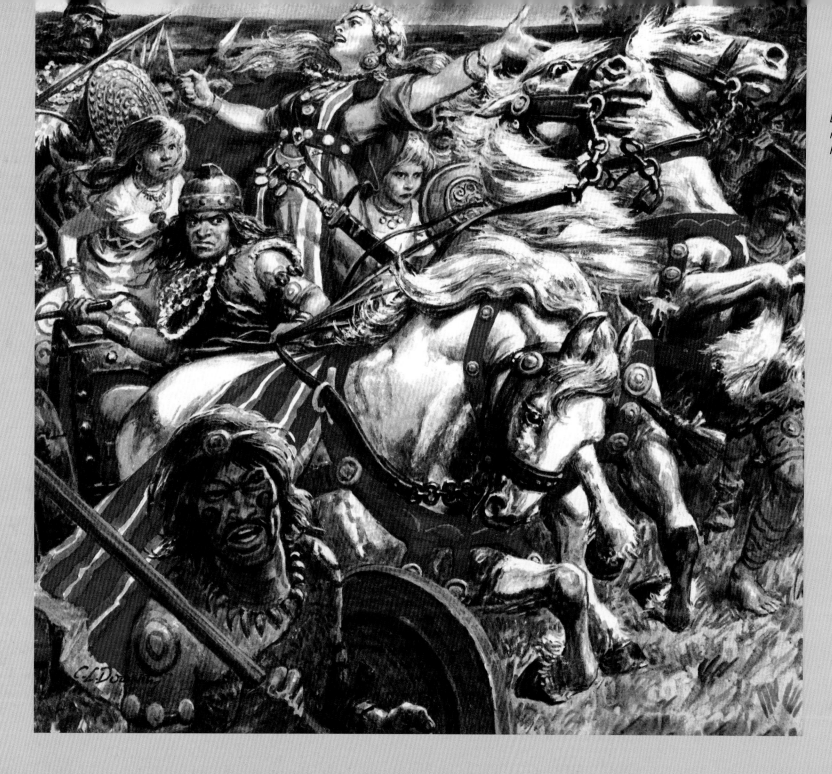

Boudicca leading the
revolt against
Roman rule

The Land

By the time of the Roman invasion, an agricultural landscape of fields and hedges was well established throughout the Thames Valley and this intensified, as Britain was fully absorbed into the Roman Empire (7).

The Romans gave the river the name Tamesis which was possibly the latinisation of an earlier British name. In AD 47 they founded London adjacent to the Thames, a town that was peopled from inception by outsiders. However, although the term Roman defines the period, there was not a sudden influx of citizens of Rome to govern the land. The "Romans" who now controlled Roman Britain were more typically provincial "Romans" from Gaul. Over time the wealthier indigenous people, including the Atrebates aristocracy, moved into the new towns, learnt Latin, wore togas and become increasingly Romanised (4).

The People

As the Romans systematically consolidated their influence, life for the majority of the population remained unchanged (4). Most settlements such as Coldharbour remained as a cluster of round houses and granaries and their life continued to evolve around the annual agricultural development of the land and the production of grain, vegetables, milk, meat, wool and leather.

Farmers living in the border zones enjoyed a period of relative stability and the opportunity to cultivate their lands without fear of border raids and the all-consuming dread of enslavement.

They must, however, have been disturbed from their most quiet sphere by the rough torrent caused by Boudicca's rebellion in AD 60-61. Under her leadership an army numbering as many as 230,000 warriors from the Iceni of East Anglia and the Trinovantes of Essex, revolted against Roman brutality.

Encouraged by the sacking of Colchester they marched on London. A maelstrom of violence and plunder ensued, resulting in the citizens being massacred and London being burnt to the ground. At night the burning town would have been visible from the high ground of what is now Richmond Park, and word of the wanton destruction would have quickly passed down through the river settlements.

The rampant tribes swept through Putney, Brentford and Staines (4) and continued west until a Roman army clinically arrested their advance and ruthlessly massacred as many as 80,000 of the warriors and their women.

The Coldharbour settlement escaped their unwanted attention by being, for once, on the right side of the river, though the proximity of the rampaging warriors must have been a little unnerving!

A Change in Climate

During this period, a change in climate had a major impact on the Thames Valley. The 1st century AD was a period of cooling temperatures and increased rainfall. Globally, the average temperature dropped by about 1°C, causing the polar ice caps to expand. As a result the sea level began to fall and continued to do so throughout the period reaching up to 1.5 m below the present level. This would have resulted in a lower tidal reach up the Thames (7). The disadvantage is that it would have been more difficult for vessels to travel up river past the tidal head. On the other hand, more riverside settlements would have freshwater flowing down the Thames without contamination from the brackish water coming up the river with the tide.

Development of a Road System

With the benefit of prior experience, the Roman Commanders knew that they could be more readily ambushed on the margins of the rivers and the tributaries. Consequently, wherever possible, they avoided the Thames and built well-placed bridges to enable secure crossings of the river.

Roads were essential as a means of communication and trade naturally followed along these same roads. No road ran adjacent to the river and so the road network tended to avoid the Thames Valley. Nevertheless, for bulk goods such as grain, the river would continue to offer an obvious transport route (7).

Kingston, though not on the main route, would have linked into the Roman road network. There was

possibly a road leading over Kingston Hill between Kingston and Putney and another track may have run from Sheen to Ham through present day Richmond Park (4). In many instances the Romans when building their road network merely straightened and improved ancient tracks (8).

Dr Tom Greeves identifying an ancient track running through Richmond Park between Ham Cross and Ladderstile gate

A closer view of the ancient track (location 24)

The Pax Romana

The ensuing 350 years of the Pax Romana would have brought relative stability and security to the occupants of the farmstead at Coldharbour in Ham. Here, a rhythm of agricultural life following the seasons would have become established without the need to take up arms or flee to the hills at a moments notice.

The fertile arable land yielded abundant crops while cattle grew fat on the rich meadowland beside the river. The burgeoning Roman City of London was hungry to take any surplus in exchange for pottery, other foods and interesting and exotic ornaments introduced via the expanded Roman trading network.

A Roman Road through the Parish of Ham

Dr Tom Greeves leading a walk of the Richmond Archaeological Society in Richmond Park in April 2015 pointed out an ancient track running through the Park between Ham Cross and Ladderstile Gate (9).

Could this track have been the remains of a straightened Romano British road?

A Saxon Shore

The Dark Ages
AD 410 to 1066

A Climate of Insecurity and Terror

Sensing that the Province of Britannia was vulnerable, the Barbarians attacked.

In the early 5th Century the Roman province of Britannia came under siege. Angles, Saxons and Jutes from Northern Germany and Jutland crossed the North Sea to carry out raids on the East and South Coasts. Picts from Scotland raided the Northeast and Irish warriors negotiated the tempestuous Irish Sea to attack settlements in the West. With Barbarians similarly advancing on the gates of Rome, Emperor Honorius in 410 instructed that Britannia should look after its own affairs (1) (2).

The peace and stability of the Pax Romana was shattered as the Roman administration of England collapsed. The country now entered a Dark Age in which the competing Germanic groups fought for dominion, forming kingdoms and sub-kingdoms throughout the country. They brought with them their own culture and pagan religion, rejecting the progress and development that had been achieved under the authority of Rome and along with it, total repudiation of the Christian faith.

London became redundant as an administrative and military centre with its imposing buildings, monuments and road network being left to fall into ruin (3).

The existing settlement at Ham is likely to have been badly affected by the loss of demand for agricultural produce and the significant reduction in trade up and down the Thames Valley. Yet the abundant riverside land would have appeared very attractive to a new group of settlers.

Artistic impression of Roman ruins left to decay throughout the English landscape

The Ruin is a poignant elegy written by an unknown author in the 8th Century. The narrator, as he stands before the immense stone ruins of an ancient Romano British town, imagines how the towers, walls and palaces must have appeared during the thriving years of the Roman occupation, bustling with life and activity. This imagery is contrasted with the desolate state of the buildings which have long since fallen into ruin. He reflects on the fragility of human endeavour and how strange are the Wyrde ways (the ways of Fate) inflicted upon the lives of men during their short time on earth.

The poem accurately captures the descent into the Dark Ages... (4)

The Saxons

It has been traditionally held that in the early 5th century the leaders of Britannia engaged Saxon federate troops *(foederati)* as mercenaries to reinforce the Regular army and provide defence against marauding barbarians (1). In return for their service, these federate Saxon troops were provided with both money and land.

An incident subsequently documented in the Anglo Saxon Chronicle (5) recounts that Saxon mercenaries mutinied in 455 and slaughtered thousands of Britons throughout the country. Without a unified authority there followed an opportunistic migration of the Germanic people to England. Despite sporadic resistance by the Britons, the Saxons by c 600 had progressively occupied much of Southern England (6).

Left: Saxons entering deserted London

Evidence of Saxon Settlement at Ham
(location 19)

It was Ham that provided a base for one of the earliest Saxon settlements in the country at the beginning of the 5th Century. In 1945 Professor Frere discovered three early Saxon sunken huts, evidently part of an early Saxon settlement at Ham, close to the river near Teddington Lock in 1945 (6)(7).

It may be that these early settlements on the banks of the Thames in North Surrey were established by the Saxon Federate troops to defend against raiders who used the Thames as the most accessible route to penetrate deep into England. Alternatively these settlements may have been those of the earliest such marauders (1).

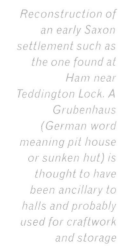

Reconstruction of an early Saxon settlement such as the one found at Ham near Teddington Lock. A Grubenhaus (German word meaning pit house or sunken hut) is thought to have been ancillary to halls and probably used for craftwork and storage

Within the site of the huts were found a number of bronze objects, a 5th Century carinated pedestal bowl and various sherds of Germanic style pottery brought by settlers, newly arrived from the Continent (6) (8).

In 1950-1, Hope-Taylor at the same location found another sunken hut evidently part of the group and more pottery (9). The pottery discovered includes 82 pieces from the Saxon period. Also of interest is a worn rim from an Argonne ware bowl and other decorated vessels.

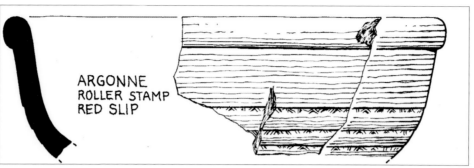

ARGONNE ROLLER STAMP RED SLIP

A worn rim from an Argonne ware bowl with bands of roller stamping and an overall orange red slip. Suggested early 5th Century dating from the Roman period but maybe this bowl was brought with the Saxons to the settlement at Ham

Argonne red ware imported from near Rheims. This sherd comes from a bowl decorated with distinctive roller stamped geometric patterns. The roller would have been engraved to make a pattern and used on leather-soft clay before firing

Below: Other decorated Vessels

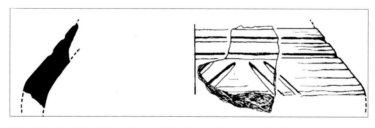

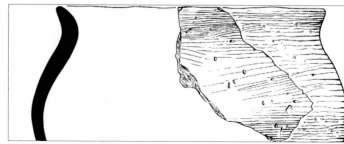

Left: A 5th Century carinated pedestal bowl (10" high) similar to the one found at Ham

Above, above right and right: Simple jars with a slightly everted rim and a hollow neck

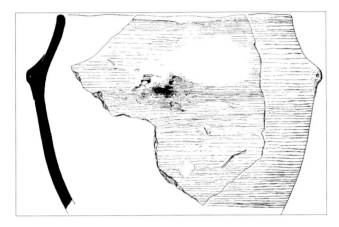

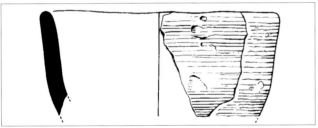

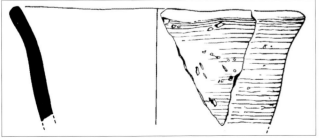

Above: A large jar

Left: A jar with a small applied boss on its shoulder that is pierced horizontally with a very small hole

Left and below: Cups or small bowls

Top right: A Saxon Loom showing the loomweights at the base, holding the threads under tension.

Also found at the site were loomweights providing evidence of weaving and the bones of cattle, pigs and sheep (6).

Although appearing simply as broken pieces of pottery these sherds provide meaningful evidence of the daily pattern of life of people in one of the earliest Saxon settlements in England. They give us a direct connection to a small community of people preparing food, eating, drinking and spending time together by the river in Ham some 1,500 years ago.

Throughout this period the Anglo Saxon chronicle records great battles and much slaughter between the Saxons and Britons (5).

It is possible that Saxon invaders took over existing or deserted Romano British farms such as the one at Coldharbour at Ham and built the farmstead itself some distance to the south next to the river (10). Alternatively, existing British farmers could have co-existed with the Saxon newcomers and adapted to their way of life (11). Nevertheless, although it was possible for the Britons to be rich freemen within this new society, it is likely that they had a lower status than that of the Anglo-Saxons.

Language and Belief

The early pagan Saxons could barely read or write and their history and traditions were passed on orally from generation to generation.

Evolving from Northern Europe, the Anglo-Saxons worshiped similar gods to the Norse and other Germanic peoples. They worshiped a multitude of pagan gods, each god controlling a different aspect of everyday life. Nature was a key part of their religion. Large rocks, special trees and other natural features throughout the landscape served as sacred shrines to the gods. Festivals celebrated by Christians at Christmas (Yule) and Easter originated from pagan festivals. The Easter Bunny symbolised fertility and coloured eggs represented the sunlight of Spring.

The Wergeld: The Anglo-Saxon settlers brought with them the Germanic blood-feud, whereby the relatives of a murder victim were expected to exact revenge. This led to extensive bloody and futile feuds. The wergeld (man-price) set a monetary value on each person's life according to their wealth and social status with a view to providing financial compensation and reduce the need for a revenge killing. Supporting this was a schedule of compensation for various kinds of bodily injuries (19). Under seventh-century Kentish law, the sum of 12 shillings was payable for cutting off an ear, 30 shillings for disabling a shoulder, and 50 shillings for putting out an eye. Murder required payment of the wergeld, a sum which varied according to social class and gender. Slaves had no wergeld, as offences against them were taken to be offences against their owners.

Anglo Saxon villages were often named after leaders or a feature in the surrounding landscape. It is the Saxons that gave Ham its name referring to land contained within the bend of a river (17).

Teddington was known as 'Tudinton - the settlement of Tudda's people'. *Surrey* derives from the Saxon for "southern region" (of a larger Thames Valley territory extending as far as Reading). *England* also derives from the Saxon word 'Angle-Land'.

In later years a rich artistic culture would flourish under the

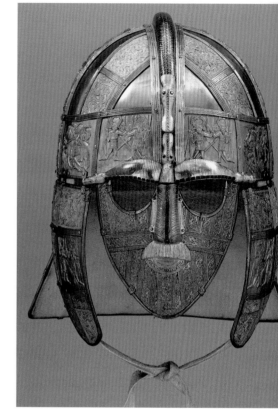

A Saxon Helmet showing the skilled metalwork of Saxon craftsmen

Four days of the week are named after early Saxon Gods, with *equivalent gods* in Scandinavia.

Tuesday	Tiw (*Tyr*), the god of war
Wednesday	Woden (*Odin*), the chief of the gods
Thursday	Thunor (*Thor*), the god of thunder, who rules the storms and sky. His symbol, the hammer, was worn by many common people for protection.
Friday	Frige (*Frigg*) wife of Woden and the goddess of love

Anglo-Saxons, producing epic poems such as *Beowulf, The Ruin* and *The Wanderer*. The myths of the Northern Europeans featuring elves, dwarves and giants were to leave a profound influence on literature through the ages. Skilled metal workers would learn to intricately shape and decorate metals.

Christianity

The Middle Saxon Period commenced with the return of Christianity in AD 604 when a diocese was established in London. The Kings of the various Kingdoms throughout England were key to the revival of Christianity throughout the land. If the Kings converted then the common people would inevitably follow. Feeling that the time was right, missionaries were sent from Italy and Ireland to convert the pagans back to the Christian faith.

At this time the Kingdoms of Northumbria and Kent were closely allied and marital alliances between them also helped influence the spread of Christianity.

During the early to mid 7th Century, Christianity became progressively established throughout the Thames Valley and Southern England. At this time Northeast Surrey, including the land at Kingston, Ham, Petersham and Sheen (Richmond), was contested by the Kingdoms of Wessex, Mercia and Kent, all fighting for control of the south bank of the Thames (11).

The Anglo Saxon Chronicle recounts that in AD 664 the sun was eclipsed on the eleventh of May, King Egbert succeeded to the kingdom of Kent and there was a great plague throughout the country (5).

The short flight of a sparrow through a Saxon hall helped inspire the spread of Christianity throughout England. © Carrie Wild 2010

Bede in his History of the English Church and People recounts how King Edwin of Northumbria in AD 627 called a council to discuss accepting the Christian faith (25). One of the king's advisors astutely argued; "Your majesty, when we compare the present life of man with that time of which we have no knowledge, it seems to me like the swift flight of a lone sparrow through the banqueting-hall where you sit in the winter months to dine with your thanes and counsellors. Inside there is a comforting fire to warm the room; outside, the wintry storms of snow and rain are raging. This sparrow flies swiftly in through one door of the hall, and out through another. While he is inside, he is safe from the winter storms; but after a few moments of comfort, he vanishes from sight into the darkness whence he came. Similarly, man appears on earth for a little while, but we know nothing of what went before this life, and what follows. Therefore, if this new teaching can reveal any more certain knowledge, it seems only right that we should follow it."

The Kingdom of Kent briefly gained control over Northeast Surrey and in AD 666, King Egbert of Kent founded the Benedictine Abbey of St Peter's at Chertsey only to be displaced soon after by the Mercians under King Wulfhere (11)(12). At around this time Frithwald, the King of Surrey endowed the Abbey under the Abbot Earkenwald, with land in Surrey including;

"xx mansas apud Muleseie x apud Piterichesham"(13)(14)
20 hides at Molesey 10 hides at Petersham

Chertsey Abbey would have provided a cell of lay brothers to live in Piterichesham and farm the land and river for the Abbey (15). Piterichesham means a home or enclosure of Patrick (not Peter). (It was not until the sixteenth century that the village came to be known as Petersham.)

The Grave of a Saxon Nobleman and Christian Lady
(location 20)

Occupation at Ham continued through the 7th Century AD. Evidence of this was found in Saxon graves containing items of the period with an apparent Kentish and Christian influence which were located some distance to the north of the settlement beside the river. This may have been the site of an earlier Romano-British graveyard (6)(16).

Although originally documented as being found in Twickenham, a letter from the original owner confirmed that these items had been found (in 1912) on the bank of the river on the Surrey Side (17).

Left: A simple site for worship would have been established in Petersham – possibly a large Saxon cross in the open, with an adjacent stone altar

Left middle: Chaff-tempered Saxon Urn found at Ham. The bowl was made of a very common type of early Saxon pottery, which had grass or chaff mixed in with the clay. It was fired in a bonfire and was quite soft and porous

Below: Saxon sword found at Ham about thirty four inches long, made of iron

Within the grave were found;

- a chaff tempered urn
- a spearhead
- an iron sword 34½ " long and 2" broad, broken into 3 pieces. It has traces of the wooden scabbard on the blade and the guard and the grip but the pommel is missing (18).
- a shield boss (late 7th Century) of unusual shape. The point may originally have borne a knob like other examples from Kent (18).

What was the Status of the People who were Buried in Ham?

Serfs were forbidden to carry spears, which were the symbol of a free man. Only members of the nobility used swords. This indicates that the warrior buried at Ham is likely to have been of some prominence and standing, a nobleman.

Dr. Sam Lucy of Cambridge University who has written a paper on similar Anglo Saxon finds, after seeing the image of the gold pendant, commented;

"This is very interesting – it certainly looks to me as if this could fit into the general idea of cross shaped gold and garnet pendants that are a feature of later seventh century female high status costume, and which were probably Christian artefacts."

It could be that this noble lady originally came from the Kingdom of Kent, a Kingdom that briefly extended to include Ham, Petersham and Kingston. Invariably, once the King of a realm had agreed on conversion to Christianity, then conversion also quickly permeated downwards through his subjects. Although the idea of burying a body with items for the next life ran counter to Christian beliefs, the merging of burial rites indicates that the grave was *"right on the cusp of the shift from Pagan to Christian"*.

Also found at this site, and likely to be evidence of another burial, was this openwork gold pendant inlaid with garnets (above) dated to c AD 550 – 650. It appears to have had a loop attached at the back near the edge and was probably sewn onto a garment. The design is that of an equal armed cross with the arms joined by an inner circle, similar to the jeweled brooches of Kent dated between AD 550 and 650 (18).

Below: A Saxon Shield Boss found in Ham. Saxon shields, made of wood, were circular with the iron boss projecting from the centre and attached to an iron handle though the thickness of the shield.

Bottom: The spear was typically made from a seven-foot long ash, oak, hazel or alder shaft with an iron head. They were the symbol of a free man because serfs were forbidden to carry them. A slave found with a spear was beaten with the wooden shaft until it snapped

Above: In later years the Saxons would employ the Shield wall as a defensive formation against the Danes. Most of the Saxon army would have consisted of the inexperienced Fyrd — a part time militia composed of freemen. The shield-wall tactic was supposed to suit such soldiers, as it did not require great weapon handling skill. Brute force, courage and teamwork would ultimately prevail. Yet the Viking warriors whose entrance to the feasting Hall of Valhalla simply required them to die with their weapon in their hand would have presented a formidable and terrifying enemy

Mercia and Wessex fighting for Control of the Thames Valley

During the 670s Kingston, Ham and Petersham were part of the sub kingdom of Surrey under Mercian control but by the 680s the West Saxons ruled the region. The establishment of an International trading port at London from late 7th to late 8th Century encouraged an expanding population with a developing economy and this would have made a positive contribution to the local settlements.

Local Churches

In the Domesday survey of 1086, which records the settlement of Petersham under the name Patricesham, the survey's use of latin signifies an earlier church that has been restored (location 21). This church at Petersham may have been built at the same time as the first Saxon church at Kingston dating from the 8th Century. It is likely that the church at Petersham came under the control of the Kingston church, though Chertsey Abbey as the principal landowner is likely to have made an annual grant towards its maintenance and supplied lay brothers to work the land. (13).

Churches were often established near pagan sites and it is possible that the central gravel island of Kingston, where the All Saints church currently stands, was a centre of pagan worship (11). This site would have been very accessible to the Saxon settlers at Ham. It has also been suggested that the great sandstone boulder, now recognised as the Coronation stone, may have been the key feature of the island, a sacred stone adding to its allure as a hallowed place, especially if this also represented a place near to where the tide coming up the Thames reached its head (11) (10).

Although evidence of its continuous use as a Coronation stone needs further investigation, the stone itself may have subtly influenced the location of the original church and settlement at Kingston (11).

The Kingdom of Mercia dominated the Thames Valley throughout the 8th Century until the early 9th Century when control fluctuated between the Kingdoms of Wessex and Mercia. By the ninth century, the country was divided into five kingdoms - Northumbria, Mercia, East Anglia, Kent and Wessex and the Thames served as a natural border between Kingdoms. Ham found itself within Wessex looking across to Teddington in Mercia but both now followed the Christian faith.

Left: The sandstone block, similar in make up to the stones used at Stonehenge is reputed to be a Coronation stone. It stands outside the Guildhall at Kingston-upon-Thames. As a pagan sacred stone it may however have had a far greater influence on the history of Kingston

Land Ownership and Status

The main division in Anglo-Saxon society was between freemen, serfs and slaves. Below the King there were two levels of freemen, the upper class thegns (pronounced thanes) and the lower class ceorls (pronounced churls). The distinction between the two was made on the amount of land that they owned. A thegn owned at least five hides of land (a hide was defined as the amount of land necessary to provide a living for one family, around 600 acres).

A District known as "the hundred" was introduced by the Saxons and defined the amount of land needed to sustain 100 households (100 hides). The hundred was headed by a hundred eolder who was responsible for administration, justice and the supply of fighting men to form the local fyrd, a part time militia. The Kingston Hundred, which included Ham and Petersham, was to endure until the end of the 19th Century.

Serfdom and Slavery

Below the thegns and ceorls were the serfs and the slaves. Serfdom was the principal source of labour in the Dark Ages. A freeman became a serf usually through adverse circumstances or by birth. A few years of repeated crop failures, a war, or a Viking raid might leave a farmer without the means to provide for his family. In such a case, in exchange for protection and the means of survival, they could offer an agreed amount of labour or produce, or a combination of the two to a local lord. These bargains became formalised in a ceremony known as "bondage" in which a serf placed his head in the hands of the lord. To become a serf was an all-encompassing commitment and included his wife and children.

The difference between a serf and a slave is that the serf could not be sold (unless the land on which he

75

worked was sold). He also had important rights to land, home, and protection. By contrast, the slave was treated as property and had only the most limited rights. Many conquered Britons would have become slaves and warfare continued to be the most common source of slaves. In later years Saxons themselves, living in the Thames Valley, were destined to become slaves as a result of repeated Viking raids on riverside settlements. In some cases a family would sell a child into slavery in time of famine to ensure the survival of other children in the family.

Working the Countryside

Having withdrawn from the Roman towns, the vast majority of the people in Southern England lived by farming the countryside. The ceorls worked co-operatively, sharing the cost of a team of oxen to plough the large common fields in narrow regular strips. These strips were

A romantic artistic impression of a Saxon Village fair

shared out alternately so that each farmer had an equal share of good and bad land. This could have established a long-term template for the field systems that were, many years later, carefully documented in the 1841 tithe map of Ham. Much of this land was later consolidated into the large estates of wealthy lords with the additional construction of a mill to grind grain. Horses and oxen were bred for heavy farm labour and transportation.

Food and Drink

The cereals most frequently grown were wheat and rye for bread, barley for cereal and oats for animal food and porridge. Common vegetables were carrots, parsnips, cabbages, peas, beans, lentils and onions. Fruit consisted of apples, cherries and plums; and honey was a sweetener that was also used with barley to make the strong alcoholic drink known as mead. This was drunk in large quantities in preference to the polluted water of the river.

Salmon and eel were readily available in the Thames as well as ducks and geese. Pigs, cattle, goats and sheep provided meat and dairy produce. Pigs were important because they produced large litters, which would quickly mature and be ready for slaughter. Sheep were reared for their wool and meat. Cows were used for their milk and later on, for hides, meat and glue. Lamps were fueled with animal fat.

Saxon Kingston

In 838 King Egbert of Wessex held a Great Council in Kingston with the apparent objective of ceding land in the south of England to the Archbishop of Canterbury in return for his loyalty and support. This Council was attended by the King, his son Aethelwulf (the under King of Kent), his noblemen and the Archbishop of Canterbury with other senior clergymen (11) (21).

Documents from the time describe the council as taking place at *'illa famosa loco quae appeletur Cyningestun in regionnae sudregiae.'* meaning *'that famous place called Kingston in the region of Surrey.'*

The name suggests a royal estate comprising scattered settlements, possibly including a large timber hall and a church, which would probably have sat on the current site of All Saints (22).

All Saints church subsequently became the historic parish church of Kingston, whose bounds stretched at one time from Molesey to Richmond, including Ham.

Viking Raids along the Thames Valley

The Anglo Saxon Chronicle in AD832 records that "This year heathen men overran the Isle of Shepey" (5).

Viking longships making their way up the Thames past the Saxon settlements at Ham and West Molesey to sack Chertsey Abbey in 1871

From this point on the Vikings unleashed indiscriminate slaughter, destruction and terror on the inhabitants of London and struck deep into the Thames Valley. The Vikings, originally from Norway then later from Denmark, were rapacious warriors with shallow draught

The Anglo Saxon Chronicle entry for AD 871 recounts: This year came the Danes to Reading in Wessex. There was much slaughter on either hand but the Danes became masters of the field; and there was slain Bishop Heahmund, with many other good men. King Alfred fought against all the Danes with a small force at Wilton, and long pursued them during the day; but the Danes got possession of the field. This year were nine general battles fought with the army in the kingdom south of the Thames; besides those skirmishes, in which Alfred the king's brother, and every single alderman, and the thanes of the king, oft rode against them; which were accounted nothing. This year also were slain nine earls, and one king (5).

Right: The various kingdoms of England in 878. The Danelaw as recorded in the Anglo-Saxon Chronicle, is a historical name given to the part of England in which the Danes prevailed and their laws applied

AD 894: They (the Danes) took all the cattle that was thereabout, slew the men whom they could overtake without the work, and all the corn they either burned or consumed with their horses every evening (5).

Below: Chertsey Abbey was sacked by the Vikings in AD 871 when the Abbot Beocca and 90 monks were slaughtered, the Abbey raised to the ground and the lands around laid to waste

warships, which could be readily beached. They made full use of the lift of the tide to plunder London and riverside settlements. Wealthy, yet poorly defended monasteries and churches at settlements along the Thames were a magnet for Viking raids.

London was occupied by a Viking army in AD 871-2 and a little later, in AD 879, a large Viking army, that would have taken a lot of feeding, passed the winter at Fulham.

Control of London changed hands between the Saxons and Vikings a number of times. Settlements at Ham and Petersham would have been readily accessible and easy prey to the crew of a longship in search of plunder and entertainment.

Further such raids throughout the 880s and 890s would ultimately have made Kingston and surrounding settlements, including Ham and Petersham, unsustainable (3) (5) (11).

The Feasting Halls of Valhalla

The Viking warriors were not overly concerned with death. Their priority was to ensure that, if they were defeated in combat, they died with their weapon in their hands. This, so they believed, guaranteed them entry to the feasting halls of Valhalla.

A Middle Saxon Period Settlement in Richmond Park
(location 22)

This must have been a very good reason to establish a small settlement on high ground, well away from the River Thames.

In the early 19th Century twelve loomstones were found at the top of Broomfield Hill in Richmond Park by the Deputy Surveyor of the Park, Edward Jesse. These provided evidence of a possible settlement during the Middle Saxon period (23) (24). Such a settlement would have been a reasonable distance from the river valley with good all round visibility and the opportunity to receive early warning of Viking longships riding the tide up the Thames. Fresh water would have been available from the Beverley Brook at the base of the hill as well as the many streams feeding down to the brook from the high ground.

Art in Nature at the base of an ancient oak at the top of Broomfield Hill near the site of a Middle Saxon period settlement

Below left: One of the loomstones from the Middle Saxon period found in Richmond Park

It was not until the early 10th century that the Danes in the south were defeated and their territories annexed to Wessex (11). Only now could farmers re-establish settlements along the Thames close to London without living in perpetual fear of sudden devastating raids.

Kingston, the Coronation Town of Saxon Kings

Kingston in the 10th Century was still little more than a rural settlement with a simple church on a central gravel island where the All Saints Church stands today (11). It has been popularly held that up to eight Saxon Kings were crowned at Kingston. Historic evidence firmly supports two of the coronations (11)(17).

- 900 AD - Edward the Elder, son of Alfred the Great
- **925 AD - Athelstan, grandson of Alfred the Great**
- 939 AD - Edmund I
- 946 AD - Eadred
- 956 AD - Eadwig
- 973 AD - Edgar
- 975 AD - Edward the Martyr
- **979 AD - Ethelred the Unready**

Bernard Cornwell the acclaimed author of "Death of Kings" part of the "The Warrior Chronicles" places his lead character, the pagan Lord Uhtred, in charge of the guard at the Coronation of King Edward at Cyninges Tun, the King's town. Uhtred observes, that because of its proximity to London the Danes had repeatedly plundered the town.

A fragment of a Saxon cross, housed in All Saints, possibly formed part of a larger cross erected to commemorate one of these coronations (16).

Athelstan meaning "noble stone" (894 –939) was King of the Anglo-Saxons from 924 to 927 and King of the English from 927 to 939. Modern historians regard him as the first King of England and one of the greatest Anglo-Saxon kings.

As a child, Athelstan had been brought up in the care of his aunt, Aethelflaed, Lady of Mercia and daughter of Alfred the Great. Following the death of his father Edward, Athelstan was immediately accepted by the Mercians as King. His half-brother Ælfweard may have been recognised as King in Wessex, but died within weeks of their father's death. Athelstan encountered resistance in Wessex for several months, and was not crowned until 4th September 925 at Kingston upon Thames. Kingston may have been chosen owing to its strategic location on the border between Wessex and Mercia and as a symbolic act of uniting the two kingdoms under the new King.

Athelstan was crowned by the Archbishop of Canterbury. For the first time his coronation service laid out the responsibilities of both the King and his people and the Christian hymn Te Deum was sung as it was at the coronation of Queen Elizabeth II in 1953. This was also the first time that a King was crowned.

In 927 Athelstan conquered the last remaining Viking kingdom centered on York, making him the first Anglo-Saxon ruler of the whole of England. Athelstan, annexed Northumbria from the Vikings and forced the submission of the Kings of Wales.

In AD 933 Athelstan established his Court in Kingston to issue grants of land to Chertsey Abbey (21). The Kings Court was not maintained in a single location but moved around the country to reinforce contact with the people and understand them better. This was essential in a country of traditionally shifting alliances and conflicts.

At the Battle of Brunanburh in 937, an epic battle during which both sides sustained dreadful losses, Athelstan's army defeated an alliance of the Scots, Danes, and Vikings to unequivocally reinforce his position as the King of all England and shape the geographic boundaries which have lasted to the present day. He never married, and was succeeded by his half-brother, Edmund in 939.

King Edgar held a council in Kingston in AD 967 to confirm privileges and land including 10 (mansiones) at Petersham to Chertsey Abbey. He held another council at Kingston in AD 972 (21).

In AD 975, Edgar died while still only in his early thirties. He left two surviving sons, Edward (the eldest) and his half-brother Ethelred. Edward was crowned king but three years later he was assassinated by one of his half-brother's retainers, with the connivance of Ethelred's stepmother.

Athelstan, c.895-939 presenting manuscripts. He gave generously to churches throughout England

Ehelred was crowned in 979 at Kingston, and although he reigned for thirty-eight years, one of the longest reigns in English history, he earned the name "Ethelred the Unready", as he proved incapable of countering the Viking threat. True translation, however, should amend *Unready* to *ill advised*.

Ethlered established a Danegeld which was a tax on the Saxon settlements to pay as tribute to the Viking raiders for not plundering the landscape. That tribute "harassed" all the people of England for the period of his reign. The Danes willingly took the Danegeld with one hand and continued their ravaging of the English countryside with their weapons in the other. Then they came back for more!

Tributes paid to the Danes;

AD 991 -   £10,000

AD 994 -   £16,000

AD 1002 - £24,000

AD 1007 - £36,000

AD 1012 - £48,000

Under the yoke of the Danegeld, which was meant to provide them with relief from the devastating Viking raids, the riverside settlements lived in a perpetual state of uncertainty and fear. The Danish raiders scoured the landscape killing any who opposed them, raping women, and seizing

An overly colourful depiction of a Viking raid. Reality would have been a little more grubby and bloody!
The Viking Scourge unleashed indiscriminate slaughter, destruction and terror to the settlements throughout England

both women and children as captives to be sold into slavery overseas. Their final wanton act of destruction was invariably to torch the thatch of the farmsteads and kill the sick and elderly who could not be sold into slavery. The pall of smoke over the countryside marked their trail through the landscape, their progress only slowed by the encumbrance of the seized women,

children, cattle and grain. Even if a farmer and his family managed to escape the vicious raids, the loss of cattle and reserves of grain would most likely force them into bondage as a serf with a local lord to avoid starvation. Many of the settlements would have been required to supply men to fight in the Saxon part-time army called the fyrd but the experienced Viking warriors would

have been a formidable foe. The Priests and lay brothers of the Kingston Minster and the Petersham Chapel would similarly have lived in perpetual fear of the irresistible lure of their poorly defended churches, resplendent with gold and silver ornaments and candlesticks, so vulnerable to attack by the crews of the Longships (5) (11).

The End of the World

Danish raids commenced a year after Ethelred's Coronation and the years around the millennium of AD 1000 were believed to herald the end of the World (11). The Viking scourge intensified through 1009 -11 as the predatory army of Thorkell the Tall, devastated the towns and villages of Surrey and south-eastern England bringing untold terror, misery and destruction on the unfortunate inhabitants.

The misery neared its finale in 1016 when Ethelred died and was succeeded by his son Edmund (Ironside). Edmund mounted a final and spirited campaign to revive the defence of England. He raised an army in Wessex and after lifting the Viking siege of London defeated a Danish army near Brentford. The Danes, under the command of Cnut, renewed their siege of London and finally won a decisive battle in Essex on 18th October 1016.

The two Kings negotiated a peace, dividing the country between them. Edmund retained Wessex while Cnut took Mercia and Northumbria. On the death of Edmund one month later, possibly from wounds incurred in the final battle, Cnut became King of England.

It has been suggested that Cnut, who was a Christian, rebuilt the church at Kingston, which had been destroyed by Viking marauders (11).

Following the death of the son of Cnut in 1042, the House of Wessex was restored under Edward the Confessor. The Royal Estate at Kingston now reverted from Danish to English ownership (11) and Chertsey Abbey continued to be, locally, the largest owner of land including Petersham.

By the 1060's, despite years of conflict, England had established a thriving economy with a centralised efficient administration, a strong well-trained army and a wealthy and well-supported church. Paradoxically, despite the success and legacy of Saxon Kings such as Alfred and Athelstan the era was to conclude with the ascent of the Vikings, albeit, Christian Vikings.

Edward ruled until his death in 1066 when he was succeeded by Harold Godwinson, who was to be the last Saxon King.

A problem now arose because Edward in 1051 had named William, Duke of Normandy, a distant cousin, as his rightful heir!

In 1066 at the Battle of Hastings, William, a Norman King, of Viking descent, with the support of the French nobility, defeated King Harold. It took William a further ten years to consolidate his kingdom, during which any opposition was ruthlessly suppressed.

Left: Ethelered the Unready (ill advised)

The Normans were descended from Viking raiders and pirates from Denmark, Iceland and Norway. In 918 under the leadership of Rollo they swore allegiance to King Charles III of West Francia in return for lands between the mouth of the Seine and what is now the city of Rouen. In exchange Rollo agreed to end their brigandage, and provide the Franks with protection against further Viking incursions.

The area is now known as Normandy. (Norman derives from Norseman).

The end of Saxon Rule

As the era of Saxon ruled England came to a close, the Kingston Hundred contained within its boundaries the settlements of Ham, Petersham, Shene (Richmond), Kew, Coombe, Chessington, Tolworth, Long Ditton, Thames Ditton and Malden.

Kingston itself remained a small rural settlement with a prominent church that serviced outlying farms such as Ham, and supported outlying chapels including those at Shene and Petersham (11).

Despite the unremitting turbulence, terror and indiscriminate slaughter that characterised much of the Dark Ages, farming life endured within ancient field systems at Ham, Petersham and Kingston. The fields were now arranged into more regular strips of land, but they continued to be ploughed each year and the lush meadowland continued to be used for grazing animals.

The people of the land spoke a Saxon language and followed a Christian religion, though undoubtedly they would have maintained many pagan rituals. A new era dawned, characterised by a structured and obedient society, which was set to provide a foundation of stability throughout the Thames Valley and the country as a whole. Yet life for the Saxon Lords was about to dramatically change.

A 1911 Sketch map of Kingston Hundred showing the thousand year legacy of the Saxon division of land

Lords of the Manor

The Recasting of Saxon England

Maintaining momentum after the Battle of Hastings, William quickly advanced his victorious Norman army through Kent into Surrey and defeated an English force at Southwark. They then continued westwards south of the Thames before crossing the river on a circuitous march to enter London from the North-west. This was a time for the people of Shene, Petersham, Ham and Kingston to maintain a low profile and avoid the depredations and "wasting" of a conquering army!

Ruthlessly consolidating his position, William built a network of castles around the country as secure bases for his army and then embarked on a fundamental transfer of land and power from the Anglo Saxon Lords to his Norman and French nobles. Although daily life changed little for the common people, the Saxon Lords of England, were systematically killed, exiled, or reduced to the peasantry (1). Yet following the invasion, most slaves, mainly oxherds and ploughmen, were given smallholdings to work as serfs, allowing them to earn a wage and maintain families, a step up from slavery but still not free.

Anglo-Saxon cathedrals and abbeys of any significance were demolished and replaced with Norman-style architecture (2).

At the time of the Conquest the largest landowners in Surrey were Chertsey Abbey and the now deceased King Harold.

Top: Norman Shield Wall

Left: The Norman army advancing through Surrey

England became a tri-lingual country with Anglo-Saxon spoken by the common people, Latin by the Church, and Norman French by the administrators, the nobility, and the law courts. Over time, most of the

By the time of the Domesday survey in 1086 only one significant Saxon landowner remained; the brother of the last English Abbot of Chertsey. At this time the largest landholding in Surrey, as in many other parts of the country, was the expanded Royal Estate.

The Doomsday Survey of 1086

Following the upheaval of the Conquest and the wholesale transfer of landed estates from Saxon to Norman and French nobles, William needed to ensure that the inheritance and rights of the Crown had not been neglected. There was evidence that in the haste of the land grab, some of his loyal Norman Lords and Barons had overlooked their rightful obligations and loyalty to the Crown and there were too many local rebellions and territorial boundary disputes for his liking.

King William confronting his Barons and demanding their fealty as well as their taxes!

The Domesday survey was initiated to establish a clear and definitive survey of land and property holdings across the country. This provided William with a sound appreciation of the nature and financial value of his Kingdom. By clearly understanding the land ownership of Saxon Lords and Monasteries and the level of taxes that had been paid during the earlier reign of King Edward the Confessor he had a benchmark for his own Norman Barons. The survey enabled William to see the extent of an individual Baron's possessions and the scale and identity of the under-tenants and knights who served the Barons. William needed to ensure the personal loyalty of the knights and under-tenants of his Lords by making them swear allegiance directly to himself and thereby preventing his Barons from rebelling against him.

Petersham appears in the Domesday Book as *Patricesham*, held by Chertsey Abbey with the following assets;
4 hides; 1 church, 5 ploughs, 1 fishery worth 1000 eels and 1000 lampreys, 3 acres (1.2 ha) of meadow. It rendered £6 10s 0d (3).

Ham and Shene (Richmond) were included within the Royal Estate of Kingston (4). Kingston was described as a vill *(village)* with 86 villagers *(villeins)* 14 small holders *(bordars)* and two serfs. With their families this would amount to a population of around 500 people (5). Kingston contained land for 32 ploughs, 40 aces of meadow and woodland. It held five corn mills three fisheries and a church (5).

Kingston remained an administrative centre for the Royal Estate and the central meeting place for the Kingston Hundred which included amongst others Petersham, Shene (Richmond) and Kew. 11th Century Kingston was characterised by a rural life of farming, fishing and milling.

The people from the settlement at Ham would have attended the church in Kingston, an important church in the area that supported chapelries at Shene, Petersham, Thames Ditton and East Molesey (5).

In the early 12th century Henry I awarded Kingston church to Gilbert the Knight. He transferred it to Merton Priory who were responsible for the church until the dissolution of the Monasteries in 1536-8 (5). It is possible that Merton Priory built a new stone church in Kingston on its present site, that became known as St Mary's Chapel.

Above: King Henry II making penance for the death of Thomas Beckett

Top right: A 13th Century image of Maurice de Croun

1154 - 1189: King Henry II. He came to the throne at the age of 21 and ruled for thirty-four years. With the responsibility of ruling a greater part of France than the French King he spent only fourteen of these years in England. Yet, during that time he managed to gain everlasting notoriety as a result of his quarrel with Thomas Becket, the Archbishop of Canterbury, resulting in the murder of the Archbishop in his Cathedral on 29th December 1170.

Official Recognition of Ham

The earliest discovered reference to Ham occurs in 1166 in accounts of money paid into the Royal exchequer of Henry II. It lists " a pasture of Ham" that had been forfeited by Robert Belet (4).

In 1168 Hamme made a generous contribution of 13s 4d towards the marriage of King Henry II's daughter Matilda (6).

In 1173 Henry II granted land in Ham to the value of £6 to Maurice de Croun, a powerful Norman baron of Anjou (4). *(From 1152 the Lords of Anjou had become subjects of Henry II and, under his standard were obliged to fight against France).* Maurice had previously demonstrated his loyalty to the King in the siege of Thouars before spending several years on Crusade in the Holy Land. In 1174, following the revolt of the sons of Henry II

against their father, Maurice remained loyal to the King. Commanding the house of Anjou, he captured Chantoceaux and Sablé, and two neighbouring fortresses.

On his death in July 1190, the Manor of Ham passed to his son-in-law Guy de Laval who presumably gained the Manor as part of his marriage dowry (4). Annual rent was paid by Guy de Laval until 1203 (the fourth year of the reign of King John) when 17s 11d was paid for the rent of Ham.

However, it appears that Guy de Laval then took part in a rebellion against King John resulting in the loss of Normandy to the English Crown. King John responded to this act of treason by confiscating his lands (4).

In 1205 the King granted the residue of the Manor of Ham to Roger de Mowbray, who already enjoyed a rent of £4 there by virtue of a previous grant of land in the Manor (4). There is an irony here that Roger's elder brother William was one of the 25 rebel barons who coerced King John into signing the Magna Carta in 1215. This may have influenced King John's subsequent decision to transfer the tenancy of the Manor of Ham to Eustache de Courtenay and men of the manor before being restored to Peter, son of Maurice de Croun.

Because of the growth of the population of the Kingston Parish it became increasingly difficult for those who lived in outlying settlements to attend the church. In 1211 an agreement was reached between Merton Priory and Kingston Church for a special chaplain, appointed by the vicar of Kingston, to be maintained at Petersham Chapel to carry out baptisms and hold services three times a week (5).

In 1220 the land of the Manor of Ham transferred to Peter's brother and heir, Amauric de Croun though his title to the land was not fully resolved until 1222. Yet in 1225 the land was once more seized by the Crown and handed over to the Bishop of Chichester, Ralph Neville, a loyal servant of King Henry III (4). As keeper of the Great Seal of England and subsequently as chancellor, Neville was noted for his impartiality. Yet in 1238 after arguing with the King, Neville was deprived of the Great Seal. Nevertheless, he continued to hold the title of chancellor until his death. He died in February 1244 in his London palace, built on a street later renamed Chancery Lane in honour of his presence there.

Above: King John reluctantly signing the Magna Carta

Three months later his lands in Ham were conceded for life to Imbert de Salinis to hold in return for annual payment of a bow of dogwood. In 1248 Imbert granted a five years' lease of the Manor to Peter de Genevre (7).

Peter de Genevre was the eldest son in the family of Humbert, count of Geneva by Agnes the sister of Thomas, count of Savoy. He was a great favourite of King Henry III and served as one of his household knights. Though dispossessed of his inheritance by his uncle, fate benefited him with the King's favour during the turbulence of the 1240's period and the 'great mortality' of the Earls and Barons of the realm. This Royal patronage enabled him to marry Matilda de Lacy, one of the wealthiest heiresses of the time descended from a family with significant landholding in Ireland, Wales and England. Matilda, was essentially the fortune-maker of a penurious but much favoured aristocrat (8). But by 1253 it appears the Croun family were back in favour, maybe by virtue of the fact that Maurice de Croun had married Isabel the half sister of Henry III. On the death of her husband Isabel was granted the wardship of the Manor (7).

The Manor of Ham

A surviving record of the Manor of Ham, produced on 23rd April 1253 shows for the first time the names of some of the people of the Manor. The Manor included 200 acres of arable land, 7½ acres of meadow and Common pasture land which could hold 200 sheep. The Manor also included one weir in the Thames valued at £1 6s 8d (4).

Fixed rents within the Manor were paid by

Philip de Hammes	7s 4½ d
Gilbert & Robert Bun	5s 4d

Smaller rents for pieces of land

Peter Toly	12d
John Faber	2 ½d
Lenered	1d
John the Clerk	a hen worth 1d
John the Netiare	a hen worth 1d
Will Emmesman	a goose worth 3d

On her death, Isabel de Croun was succeeded as Lord of the Manor of Ham by her son Maurice de Croun, a Knight of the province of Anjou. The Croun connection came to an end in 1271 when Maurice sold his holdings in Ham to Bishop Sir Robert Burnell (4). A further survey of the Manor of Ham was compiled and this disclosed the annual value of the Estate to the Lord of the Manor (4).

Above: King Edward I and Queen Eleanor depicted on an early 14th Century Manuscript

Worth   (A mark is a measure of weight of gold or silver)

Arable land in demesne	4 marks a year
Meadow	2 marks a year
A Fishery	1 mark a year
Rents	44s ½ d
One goose & two hens	4d
105 days of customary work	8s 9d
35 days of customary work for hoeing	17½ d
Carriage of corn in autumn	2s 0d
The Villeins plough 25 acres and their labour is	6s 3d
Total	**£7 16s 2d**

1272 - 1307: King Edward I. Eldest son of Henry III. Edward 'Longshanks' (so called because he was over 6ft tall) fought wars against the Scots King Robert the Bruce and was called 'the hammer of the Scots'. Edward formed the Model Parliament in 1295, bringing together the knights, clergy, nobility and burgesses of the cities.

King Edward succeeded to the throne in 1272. Robert Burnell initially served Prince Edward prior to him becoming King. When the Prince went on the Eighth Crusade in 1270, Burnell stayed in England to safeguard the Prince's interests (9).

Image of Robert Burnell

Following the death of King Henry III, with Edward remaining on crusade, Burnell went on to serve as Regent, effectively "occupying the King's place in England". He was twice elected Archbishop of Canterbury, but his personal life, which included a long-term mistress and as many as five children born out of wedlock, prevented his confirmation by the Pope. In 1274 Edward appointed him

Lord Chancellor and in 1275 Burnell was designated Bishop of Bath and Wells (9).

During his term as Chancellor, Burnell helped with the administrative, legislative and legal reforms of Edward's reign. Burnell went abroad on diplomatic missions for Edward, and for a time governed Gascony. He continued to enjoy the King's trust until his death in 1292 (9).

A Great Crusader Knight, Sir Otto de Grandison

In 1275 Burnell sold both Ham and Shene to another loyal supporter of King Edward, the Swiss Knight Sir Otto de Grandison on the condition that if Grandison were to die childless, the Manors would revert to Burnell. His Lordship of the Manor of Ham was to endure 52 years, a remarkable period for a Crusader knight who lived by the sword and ultimately died by the sword. This same year Otto, commanding 2000 English soldiers, crossed the Menai straits and captured Anglesey, the granary of Llywelyn, the last Prince of an

Independent Wales, and thereby forced his submission to King Edward and the English Crown (9).

Otto had originally come to England to serve as a pageboy in the Royal Court. He became a friend and confidante of Prince Edward and in 1269 he accompanied the Prince on the Ninth Crusade to Acre, the centre of the Christian state in the Holy Land.

On the base of the tomb of Queen Eleanor in Westminster Abbey are remains of a painting showing outlines of figures including four pilgrims praying and a knight, Sir Otto de Grandison, kneeling before the Virgin and Child. He is identified by his armorial surcoat

During this Crusade, Prince Edward was attacked by an assassin and although he managed to kill his assailant, he was struck in the arm by a poisoned dagger. It has been proposed that Otto sucked out the poison and thereby saved his master's life (9)

In 1278 Otto accompanied the former Lord of the Manor of Ham, Robert Burnell the Chancellor of England, to reform the government of Gascony. He was also employed as a diplomat, responsible for maintaining good relations with Kings throughout Western Europe (9). In 1290 Otto embarked on a second crusade to the Holy Land and granted Burnell ownership of the Manor of Ham pending his return. It is believed that following the death of Edward's wife Queen Eleanor in the same year, an image of a knight, believed to be Otto, offering prayers for her soul in the Holy Land, was featured at the base of her tomb in Westminster Abbey (10).

During the siege of Acre in 1291 he commanded the English knights in Palestine. On 15th April, supported by the Knights Templar, Otto launched a surprise night-time raid against a Saracen camp. During the raid the Knights' horses became tangled in the ropes of the enemy tents and many of the knights were killed. Otto saved the life of the Templar Commander and they managed to escape. Following a sustained siege, the Saracens destroyed the city and massacred the inhabitants. Otto escaped with his life and little else before making his way to Cyprus.

The fall of Acre signaled the end of the Jerusalem crusades (9).

Restoring a Knight's Fortune

On the death of Burnell in 1292 an inquest into his property holding recorded that the Manor of Ham held:

The Siege of Acre. The Hospitallers defending the walls in 1291

220 acres of arable land,
11½ acres of meadow,
Several pastures,
One dovecote,
One weir and a half weir,
One windmill.

The rent of tenants was 41s 7¼ d with a total value of £9 17s 11¼ d (4). This would have helped to restore the finances of a Crusader Knight who returned penniless from his Crusade in 1293 to recover his Manors in Ham and Shene.

In 1298 Otto accompanied the Knights Templar and the Knights Hospitallers to Cilicia (an ancient Kingdom now in Turkey) to fight off an invasion by the Egyptian Mamluks.

In 1307, on the death of Edward I, Otto retired to his castle of Grandison by the Lake of Geneva but remained in the service of the Crown. He rented his Manor of Shene to the Prince of Wales (later King Edward II) but retained his interests and his rents from the Manor of Ham.

In 1328 at the age of 90, Grandison travelled to Avignon to assist some friends who were under siege. He was attacked, robbed and murdered. The Pope instructed that his tomb be placed in the Notre Dame Cathedral in Lausanne, overlooking Lake Geneva, and carved with a life size statue of the knight (9).

At the beginning of the 14th Century the people of England were set to experience catastrophic events that would devastate the population, throw the economy into chaos and seriously challenge the Social order. The Great Famine of 1315-17 caused millions of deaths and marked a clear end to the period of growth and prosperity that had followed the Norman Conquest. A change in climate brought rain throughout the Spring of 1315. Crops failed in 1315 and again in 1316 and did not begin to recover until the harvest in 1317. It took another five years for food supplies to be brought up to sufficient levels to support a reduced population. The period was marked by extreme levels of crime, disease, mass death, and even cannibalism and infanticide. Parents were faced with the dreadful choice of deciding which members of the family were going to be fed to stay alive and who would be allowed to die.

Without a direct heir to succeed Grandison, Ham reverted to the Burnell family, to Maud Burnell and her second husband John de Handlou (4).

The Four Horsemen of the Apocalypse. As the 14th Century continued many people believed that the dreadful events that were occurring signalled the arrival of the Four Horsemen of the Apocalypse, mythical figures whose destruction of the Earth preceded the second coming of Christ and the advent of Judgement Day

Survivors in Ham

From 1332 there is a list of inhabitants of Ham with their relative assessed rent (4). Many of these named people with their families had survived the Great famine but within sixteen years they were set to run the dreadful gauntlet of the Black Death in 1348, a plague that is likely to have devastated their community.

John the smith	5s 0d
Philip Underhelde	4s 0d
John Sazyne	3s 8d
William Rykedon	3s 6d
Robert le Trottere	3s 4d
Ralph Edgar	3s 4d
Roger atte Panetrie	2s 4d
Richard Thorbarn	2s 0d
Richard le Froyle	2s 0d
William Babbe	1s 4d
Marjorie Thorbarn	1s 4d
Denis Alwyne	1s 0d
Juliana le Yonge	1s 0d
Alice Hoghes	1s 0d
Richard le Trottere	1s 0d
John Orpedeman	8d
John Thorbarn	8d

The total of assessment for Ham at this time of £1 17s 2d compares with an assessment of £1 1s ¼d for Petersham and £2 19s 9½d for Shene (Richmond).

> In 1337 Edward III made a claim to the French throne beginning a long-running costly conflict with France that became known as the Hundred Years' War. This was destined to seriously tax the people!

As the 14th Century progressed, disorder became widespread and the countryside was especially vulnerable to bandits. In 1339 a criminal gang raided and torched the local hamlet of Hartington (Hartleton) Coombe (the southern area of the former Parish of Ham within Richmond Park centred on the Old Lodge and adjacent land) (5). In 1346, a special Commission was appointed to arrest the 'roberdsmen, wasturs and draghlaches' (thieves) who were still terrorising the County of Surrey (5).

Upon the death of John de Handlou in 1346, Nicholas his second son by Maud, took the name of Burnell, and subsequently inherited the lands in Ham. However, Nicolas Burnell no longer held the land directly from the King but from the "town of Kingston" with a token annual rent of three cloves to be paid at the King's Coronation (4)

The Black Death

It is estimated that the plague took just 5 months to kill half the population of London (11). Because of the density of population, towns were hit harder than rural settlements. Nevertheless, in one year alone it is estimated that three out of ten people in Kingston and the surrounding area including Ham would have died of plague (5).

> In 1348, on the eve of the Black death (also known as the bubonic plague) the population of England stood at between 4 and 7 million. Originating in China, the plague spread west along the trade routes, across Europe and was introduced into England in June 1348 by a seaman who arrived at Weymouth on a ship from Gascony. The plague seems to have been spread by flea-infected rats, as well as individuals who had been infected on the continent. By autumn, the plague had reached London, and by the summer of 1349 it covered the entire country. People believed that the plague was the palpable wrath of God, a punishment of man for his many sins. Up to 40% of the population may have died.

Combined with the devastating impact of the great famine of 1315–17 this meant that in the more rural locations there were not enough people to cultivate the land and available resources were allocated to the most fruitful and fertile plots. Less productive land on the high ground, which is now within Richmond Park, would have been abandoned in favour of more verdant riverside land. This land in Richmond Park would never be farmed again.

Inspired by the Black Death the dance macabre was a popular image during the mediaeval period

In 1381 there was a major uprising known as "The Peasants' Revolt", which rapidly spread across the south-east of the country. The revolt was fired by social tensions generated by the devastating recurrent plagues, a breakdown in law and order, excessive taxes resulting from the ongoing war with France and a lack of a sympathetic response to these problems from the authorities.

In 1382, to compound the misery, Kingston and the riverside settlements suffered extensively from flooding.

The memorial brass of Sir Nicholas Burnell, who died in 1383, is one of the finest of the period in England. He was one of the Lords of Ham Manor

Sir Nicholas Burnell, 1382, Acton Burnell, Shropshire.

For members of the Royal family and their retainers there was also a natural incentive to live in areas of sparser population where fewer people were likely to catch diseases and die. Perhaps with this in mind King Edward III converted the Manor House in Shene to the Palace of Shene to make his home. In 1361–62 the plague returned to England, ruthlessly culling the population by around 20%.

Sir Nicholas Burnell died in 1383. This left Sir Hugh Burnell his son and heir, aged thirty-five.

At this time the Manor of Ham was recorded as containing;
100 acres of arable land
5 acres of meadow
5 acres of pasture
A weir

Total rents of 19s 6d with a total value to the estate of £3 8s 10d

The Manor remained with the Burnell family until 1415.

Shene Palace became the favourite palace of King Richard II and his wife Anne of Bohemia. But even a King could not deter the indiscriminate toll of the Black Death. Grief stricken at Anne's death from another outbreak of plague in 1394, Richard demolished the palace. The plague returned intermittently to the Kingston area during the 15th century causing untold misery with its grim reckoning.

King Henry V at the Battle of Agincourt

Evidence of a Mediaeval Manor House

In 1958 Secrett's farm, previously known as Ham Manor Farm located on the corner of what is now Ashburnham Road and Ham Street (opposite to Grey Court School) was demolished.

Demolition records dated June 1958 give us a frustrating picture of a local archaeological treasure that after surviving so long was quickly demolished and lost forever (12).

"The exterior of the house was probably of the 17th and 18th centuries with later alterations. The shape of the brick house followed the plan of the mediaeval house, which it partly encased and partly replaced. The remaining mediaeval structure consisted of part of a 3 bay hall of 15th century date together with part of the original stud walling (with wattle and daub infill) on one side of one bay including a (gothic) window of 2 cusped lights. It was clear from the timbers (of the roof) that the roof had been supported by a central collar purlin and king post. Behind the east cross wing was an additional wing of 2 storeys of c.1600."

Ham, a King's Manor and a New Manor House
(location 23)

King Henry V, after coming to the throne in 1413, engaged in rebuilding the Palace of Shene. To consolidate his estate he acquired the Manor of Petersham in May 1415 from the Abbey of Chertsey and in June he purchased the Manor of Ham from Sir Hugh Burnell for the sum of £200 (4). With his Royal

Estate in order he went on to tidy up the rest of his Kingdom and with a compact army of 1,000 Knights and 5,000 Archers he defeated the French nobility at the battle of Agincourt in October 1415.

It may be that Henry V subsequently commissioned the construction of a Manor House in Ham to provide him with Manor houses appropriate for the Royal household estate.

A 1913 Map of Ham Manor Farm. The Almshouses on Ham Street still remain and help identify the location of the original Manor house and barn opposite Grey Court School

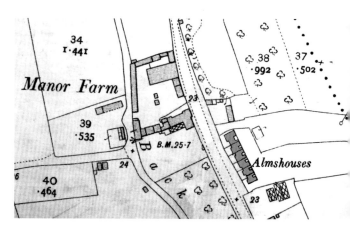

Left: The earliest photograph of Ham Manor Farm House taken in the late 1870's

Below: 1940 drawing of the barn

Tucked away in the archives of the Surrey History Centre in Woking are photographs that were commissioned by Surrey Antiquities and taken of historic Ham buildings in the 1950's. These accurately portray parts of the original Ham Manor house including the 15th Century Gothic arch that predates Ham House by nearly 200 years.

Above: The magnificent tithe barn of Ham Manor Farm

Far left: A fireplace on the first floor

Left middle: The original Gothic windows dating from c.1500

Left: Remains of a partition between the Hall and the crosswing

From the time of purchase by King Henry V until the early years of the 17th century both Ham and Petersham were treated as members of the Manor of Shene (renamed Richmond in 1501). All three Royal Manors were farmed as a combined unit and rented out to a succession of temporary Lords of the Manors. Without freehold ownership of the land there would not have been much incentive for a tenant farmer to invest heavily in buildings within the Manor and it is unlikely that they would have undertaken the construction of an expensive Manor House.

Ham remained an agricultural village throughout this period, with a mixture of grazing meadow, pasture land mostly along the river and common land. In 1416 there was a reference to a "weir by Kingston called Ham weir"(13).

In 1461, Edward IV the Yorkist King, with the help of the Earl of Warwick

By 1450 England was in crisis, facing military failure in France and an ongoing recession. More social unrest broke out, followed by the Wars of the Roses, fought between the rival houses of Lancaster under Henry VI and York led by Edward IV.

(the Kingmaker) seized the throne from Henry VI. Within the archives of the Surrey History Centre is a copy of a document titled "The Rules of Customes pertaining unto Westsheen, Petersham and Ham" established in 1465 by King Edward IV." (14).

Section XII states that the quit rent of the land at Ham and Petersham is four pence per acre, and sixpence per house. Of most interest, however, is Section III, which stipulates that on the death of a tenant:

"That which descended ought of right to descend by custom of our Manor to the youngest son and heirs, and if he had no son, to the youngest daughter and her heirs."

In 1466 King Edward IV granted the Manor of Ham along with the Manors of Petersham and Shene to his Queen, Elizabeth Woodville (depicted as the White Queen in a 2013 TV Drama).

In 1481 Edward IV confirmed a reduced toll on Kingston's inhabitants "by reason of the violent inundations and overflow of waters, lately suffered in that town…"

Below left: Edward IV c.1520, posthumous portrait from original c.1470–75

Below: Elizabeth Woodville (1437–92), Queen Consort of Edward

During the years 1469-71 Edward IV was facing rebellion from his former supporter, the Earl of Warwick who had now allied with the House of Lancaster and Warwick's cousin Lord Fauconberg. In May 1471 Fauconberg led the men of Essex, Kent and Surrey in an attack on London where Henry VI was imprisoned in the tower. Unable to reach the Tower, Fauconberg left his ships in the Thames at London Bridge and marched his army of 17,000 men on the south side of the Thames back to Kingston, intending to cross the bridge there. His campaign faltered at Kingston and he beat a retreat back along the south of the Thames to Southwark. Edward IV returned to London with his army on May 21st and that same night Henry VI died in the tower! The illuminated barge, carrying his body would have passed the settlements of Petersham and Ham making its way up the Thames for his burial at Chertsey Abbey (5).

THE BLACK DEATH

In 1486 Elizabeth had to surrender her Manors of Shene, Petersham and Ham to the victorious Tudor King Henry VII after he defeated King Richard III at the battle of Bosworth Field. Henry married Elizabeth, the daughter of King Edward IV and, by so doing, united England and set the foundation for the Tudor Dynasty and a period of prosperity and growth. Henry established his Court at Shene and changed the name to Richmond in 1501.

King Henry VIII granted the Manors including Ham to Anne of Cleves in 1540 as part of her divorce settlement. She returned them to King Edward VI in 1548.

During the winters of 1506, 1514, 1537, 1565 and 1588 the temperatures dropped so low that the Thames froze (5).

A flu epidemic in 1558 killed 20% of the population and a severe outbreak of plague tested the population further in 1593 (5).

1603 and 1625 saw further bouts of plague throughout England, which as well as causing untold fear to the local community, also devastated the local economy by restricting the movement of people and the passage of essential goods and food (5).

One local commentator wrote: *"the sickness is very much about Kingston and its neighbourhood"* and was also *"violent in London"* and *"those that go to London must not return into the country".*

The Building of Ham House

In 1607 King James I granted a 40 year lease of Ham and Petersham Manors to Sir Thomas Gorges but a year later Gorges assigned the remaining 39 year lease to George Cole of Petersham.

King James I appointed Sir Thomas Vavasour as his Knight Marshal, responsible for maintaining discipline at the Royal Court and territory within a 12-mile radius from it. In 1608, requiring a residence next to the Thames to provide easy conveyance between the Royal Palaces of Richmond, Hampton Court and Windsor, Vavasour, began to develop a leasehold estate of several acres by purchasing holdings in the Petersham Common field and other strips of land adjacent to the Eastern boundary of Ham. On this land, following an H-plan design, he built a large house with nine bays

and three storeys. The house was completed in 1610 (15).

In the same year King James I assigned the Crown ownership of the Manors to Henry Prince of Wales. Following the death of Henry in 1612 from Typhoid, the Manors were granted to his brother Charles in 1616.

In May 1617 Vavasour sold his house and estate to John Ramsay who was to become the Baron of Kingston when he assumed the title of Earl of Holderness.

After he acceded to the throne in 1627 King Charles I granted Ham and Petersham to trustees for his wife Queen Henrietta Maria. William Murray who had dutifully served as the whipping boy of the young Charles was rewarded with a knighthood and appointment as Groom of the King's Bedchamber. Murray subsequently obtained the leasehold of the Ham House Estate in 1634 from the Ramsay family (15).

Although George Cole still held the lease of the Manors of Ham and

Petersham until 1647, the Queen through her trustees, in 1631, granted a lease of the two Manors to William Murray to run for 14 years after the expiry of the term of the lease to George Cole. However, leases did not provide the security of allowing property and land to be passed down to heirs. William Murray was now very keen to obtain the freehold ownership of both the Manors of Ham and Petersham to secure his legacy. George Cole died in 1624 and was succeeded by his son Gregory.

The Making of a Royal Park – Ham Park?

Having spent much of his youth at Richmond Palace and a keen hunter, Charles I had over the years considered a large private park on the high ground above Richmond in which he could hunt deer. On acceding to the Crown he was able to realise his dream and despite advice to the contrary, on both political and financial grounds, he would not be deterred. What made this high ground so attractive was that most of it already lay within the Royal Manors of Ham, Petersham, Richmond, and Kingston. Surveys were conducted, a detailed map drawn by the surveyor Nicholas Lane and park boundaries established. Over one third (895 acres) of Ham land disappeared into the new Park along with 306 acres from Petersham, 732 acres from Mortlake, 236 acres from Putney, 117 acres from Kingston and a mere 69 acres from Richmond (17).

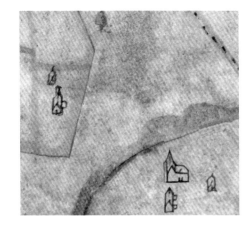

In 1635 Gregory Cole was obliged to surrender large parts of the Common land of both Ham and Petersham. He had to relinquish his home (later to become Petersham Lodge) on the North East side of the Park and his 200 acre Hartington (Hartleton) farm, part of a small Manor, which had been acquired by his father in 1603. (The farm house buildings were located just to the south west of the current White Lodge in Richmond Park near Pen Ponds Car Park).

Having been unceremoniously dispossessed, Gregory Cole assigned all of his remaining

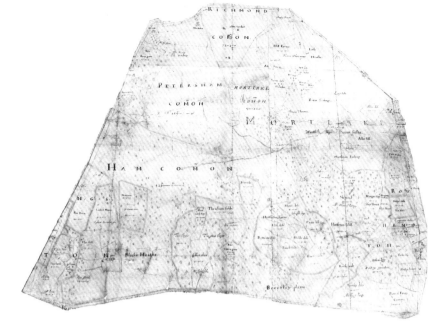

leasehold rights in the Manors of Ham & Petersham to William Murray for £2,450 and headed off for pastures new. William and his wife meanwhile embarked on a programme of refurbishment and decoration of Ham House and also with a view of expanding their property diverted the last 400 yards of Ham Street, approaching the river, 30 yards to the west (14).

The enclosure of the park was completed in 1637 and the two Cole houses were occupied by the newly appointed deputy rangers of the Park. Loanes House just inside Ham Gate was demolished.

Above: The 1632 Survey Map of Nicholas Lane showing the land holding within the planned boundaries of the proposed park

Above left: Hartleton Farm was located on the site of the Old lodge, since demolished, just to the east of Pen Ponds Car Park.
This was formerly a manor in its own right that belonged to Merton Priory. North west of Hartleton farm is Rutnells Lodge. c.1630

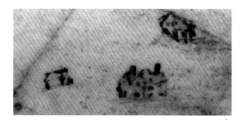

Above: Nicholas Lane's Map of 1632 showing the scale of the buildings (known as Loanes House) just inside Ham Gate

Securing the Manorship of Ham

William Murray held his first Court as Lord of the Manor of Ham on 23rd April 1637. Desperate to gain the freehold of the Manors, Murray made several petitions to both the Queen and the King but without success. Although Murray was created Earl of Dysart by King Charles, his Earldom was never formally recognised by the Parliament and the Civil War precluded the official seal (4).

In 1639 Murray transferred the title to his estates in Ham and Petersham to his wife and daughters, which enabled them to avoid the confiscation of the estates by Parliament during the Civil War. Accompanying Prince Charles he fled the country, never to return. Following the death of her mother in 1649, Ham House was made over to Elizabeth and her husband Sir Lionel Tollemache.

On Thursday 18th November 1647 there was a great rendezvous of the Army under General Cromwell near Kingston at Ham (18)

King Charles I was beheaded in 1649 and shortly after, Parliament put the Royal estates, including the Manors of Ham & Petersham, up for sale. A survey made at the time shows that: Ham comprised 254 acres and 3 roods valued at £124 3s 1d a year & Petersham held 92 acres valued at £51 6s 8d. The surveyor made a note that the remaining part of Ham Common containing 100 acres was "much better land than most of the enclosed lands in the Manor" (4).

In 1650 William Adams, on behalf of the Murray daughters, purchased the two Manors. Following the restoration in 1660 the titles derived

Portrait of the Duke and Duchess of Lauderdale. Two powerful shaker makers!

from these sales were cancelled but this did not deter them from further attempts to gain the freehold of the Manors. In 1665/66 Sir Lionel Tollemache was granted the freehold of 75 acres of land covering Ham House and its immediate grounds in trust for the Murray daughters and Sir Robert Murray was given a 61 year lease of 289 acres of land within the two Manors, also in trust for the Murray daughters.

On the death of Sir Lionel Tollemache in 1669, his widow Elizabeth, an ambitious and politically shrewd woman, wasted no time in forging a close friendship with an equally adroit political operator, John

Maitland, the Earl of Lauderdale. Shortly after the death of his ailing wife two years later, he married Elizabeth and he became the Duke of Lauderdale. A powerful Minister with the patronage of the King he skillfully negotiated the freehold ownership of the Manors of Ham and Petersham and ownership of all the property, an outcome that had eluded the Murrays for so long! (4).

On Lauderdale's death in 1682 he left, along with some substantial debts, the Manor of Ham and Petersham to Elizabeth, thereby securing the estate for the Tollemache dynasty but denying Elizabeth a life of profligacy!

The Mystery of Hatch

There are occasional references to Ham and Hatch, such as the plaque on the former almshouse on Ham Parade, but where exactly was the hamlet of Hatch?

The name Hatch is derived from the Anglo Saxon *hacche* meaning a gate. John Cloake, a prominent Richmond historian, investigated this question in detail. He concluded that Hatch was a small hamlet on the north side of Ham Common either side of the Petersham Road including the New Inn (originally in 1637 known as the Sign of the Harrow), South Lodge and the cottages leading up to Ormeley Lodge (19).

A Mediaeval Landscape in Richmond Park

Though it is unlikely to have ever entered his mind, King Charles by establishing an enclosed hunting Park, essentially froze the landscape within Richmond Park and preserved a mediaeval landscape. Dr. Tom Greeves in his 1992 survey of Richmond Park identified within the former Parish of Ham: (20)

- Ridge and furrow ploughed land, close to Ham Gate showing arable cultivation dating from the 14th Century
- The site of Loanes House, a mediaeval house with double gables and two chimney stacks located close to Ham Gate which was demolished some time after July 1637
- A Mediaeval ditched boundary, close to Thatched House Lodge which defined the boundary separating Kingston and Richmond
- A Mediaeval road crossing the south part of the Park from Ham Cross to Ladderstile gate (this was the original route to Kingston)
- Rutnells enclosure close to Pen Ponds car park with two buildings each with central chimney stacks
- The site of Hartleton farm, which was the focus of the Manor of Hartleton, held by Merton Priory from the mid 13th Century but documented as early as AD 1167 and features three buildings, one with twin Chimney stacks. This farm sat close to an ancient border between Mortlake and Ham. By implication there is a chance that there was a building here before the Norman Conquest

Right: A Mediaeval Road in Richmond Park (location 24)

Below right: Lidar image showing Mediaeval ridge and furrow just to the east of the former site of Loanes House near Ham Gate

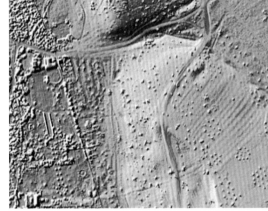

The Transformation of Rural Ham

The Changing usage of the Land

By the time that Thomas Crawter drew his immense tithe map of Ham in 1841, the village had evolved to support an agricultural community surrounding a cluster of grandiose houses. These were homes to many Admirals, Generals, Government servants, artists and traders who, with their wives, had achieved some success and wealth in various and diverse parts of the Empire. But that is another story!

Meadows and pastureland were situated mainly on the wetter land by the river and arable strips of land were worked where we now find the urban landscape of Ham and the Tudor Estate.

Hollybush, Barnfield, Fern Hill and Meadlands previously identified as the names of fields in Ham have since become the names of streets and schools in the area.

The tithe map revealed that in 1841 the total area of the Parish of Ham was 1,920 acres, made up of 964 acres inside Richmond Park for the use of Queen Victoria and 956 acres available to the people of Ham. Although the Park belonged to the Crown, taxes on lodges and gamekeepers cottages were paid to the Ham Parish (1).

At this time, Ham had three farms all owned by the Earl of Dysart: Ham Manor Farm opposite Grey Court School; Home Farm at the junction of Ham Street and Lock Road; and Church farm located on the current site of Parkleys with orchards covering most of the Tudor Estate.

The arable crops consisted of wheat, barley, oats and flax (used to make linen and an edible oil), potatoes, turnips and mangel wurzels (a type of beet used to feed cattle). In the latter part of the 18th Century the arable land in Ham Fields was converted to market gardens (1).

In 1904 eighty acres of riverside land were leased by the Earl of Dysart to the Ham River Grit Company for commercial extraction of top quality gravel (2). The Coldharbour site disappeared as the gravel workings increased to 200 acres and the ever expanding gravel pits in turn slowly filled with water. If it had not been for a number of diligent antiquarians searching for prehistoric artifacts the distant history of Ham would have vanished without trace.

The make up of Ham Land in 1841

Arable land	449 acres
Woodland	1 acre
Richmond Park Woodland	114 acres
Common land	216 acres
Pasture land	290 acres
Richmond Park Pasture Land	850 acres

Ham Street- river end 1940

Edge of Manor Farm, Ham Street 1940

Members of the Greenwood family working in Lammas Lands

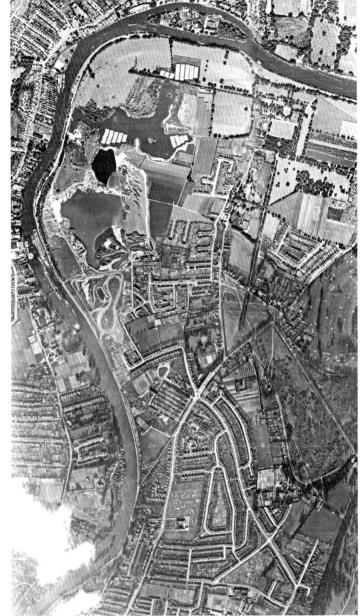

In 1925 Eric Parker published a book titled "Highways and Byways in Surrey" and includes a nostalgic recollection of Ham; (3)

I never saw Ham until one day, walking out from Kingston, I suddenly found myself in the fruitful spaces of market gardens and farms. It is the suddenest change. Kingston with the oldest memories of all Surrey towns, is as new and noisy as a thoroughly efficient service of tramways can make it; and then, within a stone's throw of bricks and barracks, you come upon acres beyond acres of level farmland, bean-fields and cabbage fields and all the pleasantness of tilled soil and trenched earth and the wealth of kindly fruits. When I saw the fields by Ham on a hot day in August there were country women gathering runner beans into coarse aprons, stooping over the clustered plants, the humblest and hardiest of workers on the farm.

Above: Cows from Ham Manor Farm passing Ham House stables. For years they competed with the 71 bus for right of way along Ham Street

A Changing Environment

During the Second World War artists were commissioned to make sketches of typical rural life throughout England. The adjoining villages of Petersham and Ham were recorded more fully than any other plot in the country. This wonderful collection of 18 sketches is now held at the Victoria and Albert Museum.

A Modern Landscape within the Parish of Ham

Following the war, many of the fields and orchards were transformed into a low density, urban network of roads, houses, schools and shops. Yet, despite this urban encroachment, Ham continues to be blessed with both the leisurely embrace of the River Thames and an abundance of woodland and green open spaces.

Left: Ham Riverside Lands

Right:Ham Common at sunrise

Far right: Postcard of Ham Common Pond c. 1900. Note the old Malt House behind the pond, which blocked access to Lock Road

Above: Ham Common pond

Ham Riverside Lands

The gravel pit wasteland was levelled, albeit at a higher level than before. Fighting plans for further housing development, the local community tenaciously safeguarded the majority of the land and helped transform the area into a local Nature reserve covering 200 acres. This natural environment boasting bee orchids and stonechats now forms a vital natural border between the river and the urban settlement and is widely appreciated for its diversity of plants and wildlife.

Common Lands

The common land of Ham, (Ham Common) on either side of the Upper Ham Road supported cows, sheep, horses, donkeys, pigs, goats, ducks and chickens and it was their continuous grazing that prevented the growth of woodland. As soon as these grazing animals departed, the woods and dense undergrowth quickly took hold, just as they did several thousands of years ago at the end of the last ice age. Though at that time, there was a multitude of wild grazing animals to keep the undergrowth in check.

Ham Common Pond

Located in the north west corner of Ham Common, the pond was originally a watering hole serving the animals that grazed on the common land. Cows were present here until 1932, oblivious to the resounding crack of leather on willow from the summer cricket matches on the green.

In recent years the pond with the careful attention of local residents has been transformed into an attractive wildlife habitat. Now it is the preserve of swans, Egyptian and Canadian geese, coots, moorhens, mallards, large carp and a solitary turtle that can occasionally be seen sunbathing on the small island in the middle of the pond.

Latchmere Brook

Water draining from the higher ground of Richmond Park flows into the Latchmere Brook (formerly known as the Lechmere) that runs along the foot of the hill. The name 'Latchmere' derives from 'lache', meaning *lazy or slow-moving* and 'mere', *a marsh or lake*. Latchmere School, House, Recreation ground, Road and Lane are all named after the Latch mere.

Now culverted for most of its course, it emerges into the light of day opposite the Park Gate house just before Ham Gate. Passing through a gap in the Park wall it meets a small stream on the West side of Ham Gate Pond and at this exact point its name is transformed to the Sudbrook, meaning the South Brook.

Sudbrook

The Sudbrook meanders parallel to the Park wall, and leaves the Parish just after entering the Sudbrook Golf course. From here it continues its journey underground through Petersham before joining the Thames near River Lane.

Top left: Latchmere Brook just outside Ham Gate

Above: Ham Gate Pond

Left: Sudbrook just inside Ham Gate

Ham Gate Pond

Overflow water from Ham Dip pond flows downhill to another enlarged pond located just inside Ham Gate. A narrow ditch trickles the overflow from this pond into the Latchmere/ Sudbrook. A patient visitor to this pond on a quiet weekday morning may be rewarded with the flash of the iridescent plumage of a local Kingfisher.

Pen Ponds

In the 17th Century a trench was dug to drain the boggy land in the Park and improve the terrain for hunting. With the removal of gravel for local construction this trench was widened and deepened to form the two ponds that we see today. Overflow water from the ponds flows down to Beverley Brook.

In earlier times eels would use available streams up to the ponds from the Thames. The ponds, which formerly lay within the Parish of Ham are now the most distinctive features of the Park, especially for passengers sitting on the left side of aircraft making the final descent into Heathrow!

Ham Dip Pond

A spring above Dann's Pond in the South of the Park near Kingston gate flows downhill through a small valley known as Ham Dip that has been dammed to form Ham Dip Pond. This was originally constructed to serve as a watering hole for deer.

Top: Ham Dip Pond near Ham Cross

Right: Olympic rings near Pen Ponds

Above: Attenborough Watering Hole.
"It's not what you look at that matters, it's what you see."

Attenborough Pond and Martins Pond

A recent addition to the landscape is the Attenborough Pond, located close to Robin Hood gate and fed by a small stream running down from Martins Pond. This pond in turn collects water from the slopes of Broomfield Hill to the south and Spankers Hill to the north. The Attenborough Pond now serves as a popular watering hole for the deer in the Park.

A Natural Environment and Extensive Recreational Resource

Despite his uncompromising pursuit of a hunting park, local residents have King Charles I to thank for putting a wall around Richmond Park and preserving an ancient landscape for posterity. A montage of woodland, heath and acid grassland in the park now supports some of the oldest oak trees in England and more than 600 red and fallow deer. Moreover, in compensation for the loss of their common land within the Park, Ham Common was transferred to the residents of Ham in perpetuity.

The surviving natural environment of Ham has become an extensive recreational resource that benefits the entire Community, all within walking distance from their homes.

Above: Stags grazing close to Attenborough Watering Hole

Below: Having fun in Richmond Park. Just behind to the left is the possible site of a pre-historic barrow

This is our Legacy, a Legacy that we need in turn to safeguard for future generations.

Legacy

The Untold Story of Ham has taken us on a long, eventful and engaging journey, including almost unimaginable hardships and violence, through to a stable, interdependent pattern of life. In recent years the development of a low-density urban environment and population within a well-preserved historical environment has made Ham a very desirable place to live.

Our own existence represents only a tiny period in the overall timescale of these historical events. However, we have a shared responsibility to both appreciate and safeguard this precious historical and natural environment for future generations.

Inevitably that responsibility tends to devolve to a few dedicated volunteers, but in Ham we are fortunate to have several groups of committed people willing to give up their time to safeguard our natural surroundings and help deter the encroachment of more intrusive and less sympathetic developments. The demolition of the Mediaeval Manor house and tithe barn was a sad loss to Ham. With increased understanding let us hope that any future development in the area will respectfully reflect our colourful and intriguing history.

Recognition and appreciation needs to be given to the active members of the following groups:

Ham & Petersham Association including the people who look after the Avenues, and Latchmere Brook
Ham Amenities Group
The Ham Pond Group
The Ham & Petersham Magazine
The Friends of Ham Lands
Ham United Group
Thames Landscape Strategy Group
The Friends of Richmond Park

They are all helping to preserve and safeguard our Legacy for future generations.

Areas for Further Investigation

Having compiled this untold story of Ham, I hope that it serves to spark interest for other people to seize on different aspects of the story and investigate or illustrate a little further. The following areas do require further attention;

1) A consolidated record of the nature and current location of all the prehistoric artefacts that have been found in Ham.
2) A permanent exhibition at Thames Young Mariners Base to clearly show the remarkable prehistoric legacy of this site and some of the many artefacts which were found here but are currently held in storerooms elsewhere.
3) Further investigation of Aubrey's Ramp running through Ham Common to get a better understanding of the age and nature of the construction.
4) A comprehensive Lidar survey of Richmond Park and Ham Common to provide an idea of locations of interest for further archaeological investigation.
5) A more detailed review of the surviving photos of the interior of the Manor House and the demolition records to build a model of the Mediaeval Manor House that existed for 500 years at Ham.
6) Recognition of Coldharbour, which was one of the original recorded settlements of Ham, a name that has long been lost to local knowledge. Hopefully the local council will officially acknowledge this name at some stage in the future.
May the Legacy Continue!

Gordon Elsden, Ham
April 2017

Thank you

A big "**Thank you**" to the following people for their help in bringing this fabulous story alive;

Chris Archer, the man who designed the album covers for "Queen"; Creativity apparently runs in the family because his Dad also won a Hollywood Oscar in 1972! Thanks for his patience and precision in establishing the original design layout of this book and his assistance with the formatting of the maps and the front cover.

Jane Baxter and her team at Richmond Upon Thames Local Studies Library for helping with the location of old maps.

Lyn Blackmore, Senior Finds Specialist at Museum of London Archaeology (MOLA) who specialises in Saxon and Medieval pottery. Lyn was especially helpful with the background of the Saxon pottery found in Ham and helped refer me to other experts for the Saxon gold pendant.

Shaan Butters; Her book *"That Famous Place – A History of Kingston Upon Thames"* was an excellent and invaluable reference to build the story during the Saxon and Mediaeval periods. She has done the hard work in establishing the detailed history of Kingston and adjacent settlements.

John Cloake. Although I will never have the opportunity to meet with John Cloake I am extremely grateful for the painstaking historical research he did on Ham during the Mediaeval period and his many articles published by the Richmond Local History Society.

Jon Cotton, who is arguably the leading authority on London's prehistory. He worked for the Museum of London, at one time heading the Department of Greater London Archaeology (West) and later as a Senior Curator. He now works as an independent archaeologist. I am extremely grateful for his patience in reading my initial draft document and giving me the benefit of his extensive experience with extremely valuable feedback.

Bob Cowie, is one of MOLA's most experienced field archaeologists. He was exceptionally helpful and prompt in providing valuable feedback on the artefacts of the Saxon period found in Ham.

Anne Dodd Manager Post Excavation Manager of Oxford Archaeology for her generous offer to use some of the fabulous images produced by them.

Nicola, Sophie and Harry Elsden for their patience and support in the lengthy investigation in all weathers of the terrain within the original Parish of Ham. Not to mention the 100 photos that were required to get one reasonable picture! Also to Nicola for the proofreading and editing of the final layout.

Eileen & Richard Elsden: My Mum and Dad for bringing me to the Parish of Ham many years ago, and introducing me to the wonderful river, common, woods and park where, with my two sisters Frances and Debbie, we had so much fun.

David Field, for his invaluable document "Ham; The Edwards Collection" published in 1983. Without it, much of the knowledge on the prehistoric period in Ham would have been lost forever.

Christiana Gilbert, for her artistic representations of the local landscape in the early prehistoric period.

Alison Graham, for her professionalism, her patience, her calmness and being good fun to work with.

John Hood, Chair of the Richmond Archaeological Society for his ongoing diligent investigation of the ramp running through Ham Common and his interest in all elements of this project.

Rose Hooker of the Surrey Archaeological Society for her assistance in helping locate obscure documents relating to the prehistoric period in Ham.

Tasha Hunter, Ecology Policy and Planning Officer of Richmond Council for her help, especially with the investigation of the ramp in Ham Common.

Dr. Sam Lucy of Newnham College, Cambridge University who provided her valuable expert opinion on the nature of the Saxon gold and garnet pendant found in a grave in Ham.

Caroline McDonald, Senior Curator of the Museum of London: For her very prompt and professional advice and guidance throughout my research of Ham during the prehistoric period as well as proving a comprehensive list of all the artefacts from Ham currently held in the Museum of London.

Natalie Mabelis, one of Ham's talented local artists, for her hand drawn pictures and her patient checking of the text of this book.

Melanie Millward, Greater London Historic Environment Record Officer, for providing a comprehensive list of prehistoric artefacts on record from the Ham area and patiently answering numerous questions.

Dr Courtney Nimura, Institute of Archaeology, Oxford for her positive feedback on the initial draft.

Vivienne Press, for her careful guidance, patience, positivity and inspiration in helping to shape this story and bring it alive. She has been a great teacher!

Christine Reynolds, Assistant Keeper of Muniments, Wesminster Abbey, who located an early 20th Century reconstruction picture of Queen Eleanor's tomb.

Charlotte Samuels, Curator, Kingston Museum for allowing me access to the various artifacts from Ham held in the Kingston Museum.

Professor Danielle Schreve, Director, Centre for Quaternary Research, Department of Geography, Royal Holloway University of London for her assistance and advice on the Paleolithic period relating to the artefacts found in the Parish of Ham.

Sarah Sinclair, Editor of the Ham & Petersham Magazine for her enthusiastic support and advice.

Vivien Sunlight, for her support and positive encouragement throughout this project.

Duncan Sutton and his colleagues at the Surrey History Centre in helping me find my way through the maze of old maps relating to Ham.

Mike Watson for his invaluable final proofreading.

Leslie Webster, formerly Senior Curator of the British and Irish Early Medieval collections at the British Museum who gave valuable feedback on the relevance of the Saxon artefacts found in Ham.

Dr Neil Wilkin, Curator, European Bronze Age collection, Department of Britain, Europe & Prehistory, The British Museum for his interest, support and very positive feedback.

Catriona Wilson of the Surrey Archaeological Society for her assistance in tracking down artefacts relating to the Saxon period in Ham.

Natascha Wintersinger, Curator, Museum of Richmond for allowing me access to the various artifacts from Ham held in the Museum of Richmond

Susan Youngs who previously worked for the British Museum and now helps out at Twickenham Museum and gave valuable feedback on the relevance of the Saxon artefacts found in Ham.

Sources of Information and Picture Credits

Introduction
1)   Sketch by Natalie Mabelis

Chapter One. Beating the Bounds

Sources of Information
1) John Cloake - The Early History of Ham (page 1) Richmond Local History
2) The Parish of Ham Tithe Map 1841 & Tithe Apportionments 1842 Surrey History Centre. See also "The London Gazette" Friday July 25th 1834 announcing the commissioning of the Church and defining the boundary of the Parish. (Pages 1392 & 1393)
3) Johnson & Wright – Neolithic Man in North East Surrey - 1903
4) John Cloake - The Robin Hood Lands, the Hamlet of Hatch. Richmond Local History Society
5) Charles Harper – The Portsmouth Road 1895
6) Collenette - A history of Richmond Park
7) Architectural notes and photographs of the Demolition of Ham Manor Farm 15/6/1958 Surrey History Centre CC32/21/12

Picture Credits
1) Map of Ham created in Photoshop by Gordon Elsden
2) The River Thames looking west to Eel Pie Island from the Ham Bank (Gordon Elsden)
3) Thomas Crawter Tithe Map 1841 – cleaned up image taken from a map held in Surrey History Centre.
4) Beating the bounds in London. Public Domain Image
5) St Andrews Church – Gordon Elsden
6) Picture of Sir Richard Owen standing next to the skeleton of a Moa. Public domain image.
7) 1880 OS Map of Ham Middlesex XX16. *Courtesy of Richmond upon Thames Local Studies Library & Archive*
8) Impression of the red roofed barn at Coldharbour by Gordon Elsden
9) Copy of antique print of Teddington Lock held by Gordon Elsden from an original study by William Tombleson and published in "Tombleson's views of the Thames and Medway" 1833-34.
10) The Olympic torch being carried through Teddington Lock – Gordon Elsden
11) Photo of the Ancient drive running through Ham – Gordon Elsden

12) Image of skeleton in Gibbett – Gordon Elsden
13) Photograph of sign at Tibbet's corner – Gordon Elsden
14) Beverley Brook – Gordon Elsden
15) The Old Lodge, Richmond Park - *Courtesy of Richmond upon Thames Local Studies Library & Archive*
16) The Solitary Cedar – Gordon Elsden
17) 1880 Map showing the Ham boundary. *Courtesy of Richmond upon Thames Local Studies Library & Archive*
18) Ham Manor Farm House *Reproduced by permission of Surrey History Centre*
19) The ancient tithe barn *Reproduced by permission of Surrey History Centre*
20) Grey Court House – Gordon Elsden
21) The Royal Oak in Ham Street. Drawing made by John Sanderson in 1940 as part of the Recording Britain Collection. *©Victoria and Albert Museum, London*
22) The Royal Oak Pub – Gordon Elsden
23) The Thames at dusk – Gordon Elsden

Chapter Two. The Thames shapes Ham

Sources of Information
1) www.thamesdiscovery.org   Thames Discovery Programme, Museum of London Archaeology
2) Fossil evidence of London's past environment. Presentation produced by the Royal Geographical Society.
3) www.naturalengland.org
4) Merriman N. - Prehistoric London by HMSO
5) Dinnis R. & Stringer C Britain – One million years of the human story. 2013 NHM
6) Sargent A. – The Story of the Thames.
7) Prehistoric Twickenham by Robert Cowie
8) TQ 1765 7135 MOLAS BHE94 refers.
9) Wymar J.J. 1987 - The Palaeolithic period in Surrey 26-7 GLSMR 020847
10) Pers comms Professor Danielle Schreve
11) David Field: Tranchet Axes and Thames Picks Mesolithic core tools from the West London Thames

Picture Credits

1) Painting by Christiana Gilbert shown in the information centre at the Windmill on Wimbledon Common. *Courtesy of Wimbledon and Putney Commons.*
2) Watercolour impression of a Megalodon
3) Sea shell fossil found in the Richmond area. *Courtesy of Museum of Richmond.*
4) Artistic impression of an ice sheet
5) Modification of a drawing showing the Thames changing its course. Archaeology of the Gravel Terraces of the Upper & Middle Thames (AGT) early prehistory to 1500BC Page 41 Fig 2.1. *Courtesy of Oxford Archaeology and the British Geological Survey.*
6) Watercolour impression of a braided river channel.
7) Cross-section showing the downward development of the Gravel terraces. Combining a sketch by M. Cook and illustrations in Archaeology of the Gravel Terraces of the Upper & Middle Thames (AGT) early prehistory to 1500BC Page 19.
8) The Thames – Gordon Elsden

Chapter Three. Predators

Sources of Information

1) Dinnis R. & Stringer C Britain – One Million years of the Human Story. 2013 NHM
2) Wymar J.J. 1987 - The Palaeolithic period in Surrey 26-7 GLSMR 020847
3) www.nhm.ac.uk/nature-online/life/human-origins/early-human-family/homo-heidelbergensis September 2015
4) *pers comms* Professor Danielle Schreve
5) Merriman N. - Prehistoric London.
6) Dinnis R. & Stringer C Britain – One Million years of the Human Story. 2013 NHM
7) Ellaby R. The Upper Palaeolithic and Mesolithic in Surrey (Accession number A18989)
8) Times article; "Homo sapiens cleared of murdering the Neanderthals" September 2014 by Hannah Devlin. Commentary by Chris Stringer of the Natural History Museum.
9) Cowie Robert - Prehistoric Twickenham (including Ham Fields)

Picture Credits

1) Map showing location of prehistoric artefacts and monuments found in and around the Parish of Ham. Produced by Gordon Elsden
2) A reconstruction drawing of a Palaeolithic straight-tusked elephant, which was created in 1995 by artist Derek Lucas. © *Museum of London*
3) A reconstruction drawing of a Palaeolithic woolly rhino, which was created in 1995 by artist Derek Lucas. © *Museum of London*
4) Photograph of the Lower Palaeolithic hand axe found in Richmond Park held as part of the Wymer collection at the Royal Holloway University. *Courtesy of Professor Danielle Schreve and the Department of Geography, Royal Holloway University of London.*
5) Reconstruction of Homo heidelbergensis in Richmond Park 400,000BP by Gordon Elsden
6) Hominins butchering a brown bear carcass on the banks of the Thames c 300,000 years ago. (AGT) early prehistory to 1500BC Page 83 Figure 3.16 Reconstruction of by Peter Lorimer Oxford Archaeology. *Courtesy of Oxford Archaeology*
7) Representation of the Thames during the Ipswichian interglacial 125,000 to 90,000 years © *The Natural History Museum | The Trustees of the Natural History Museum, London.*
8) Neanderthal hunters stalk wooly mammoths across the Thames Valley tundra c 50,000 years ago. (AGT) early prehistory to 1500BC Page 128 Figure 6.7 Reconstruction by Peter Lorimer of Oxford Archaeology. *Courtesy of Oxford Archaeology*
9) Upper Palaeolithic spearhead dating from 38.000BP found near the Coldharbour settlement in Ham. © *Museum of London*
10) Drawing of a mammoth being hunted. © Museum of London
11) Fossilised mammoth's tooth displayed in Richmond Museum. *Courtesy of Museum of Richmond.*
12) Painting by Christiana Gilbert reconstructing the terrain of Wimbledon Common and the Beverley Brook some 50,000 years ago. *Courtesy of Wimbledon & Putney Commons.*
13) A reconstruction drawing of an Upper Palaeolithic reindeer, which was created in 1995 by artist Derek Lucas. © *Museum of London*

Chapter Four. Ultimate Hunters

Sources of Information

1) Field D. Ham : The Edwards Collection Surrey Archaeological Collection. Volume 74 (1983) 169-184
2) Lacaille.A.D. Mesolithic facies in the transpontine fringes. Volume 63 Surrey Archaeological Collection.(1966) 21-9
3) Ross C & Clark J London -The Illustrated History/Penguin Books 2011
4) Merriman N. – Prehistoric London
5) David Field: Tranchet Axes and Thames Picks Mesolithic core tools from the West London Thames
6) Cotton J: Struck flints from Ham Dip Pond, Richmond Park.
7) Carpenter L.W. Some Mesolithic sites in North east Surrey - *The Archaeological Newsletter* Vol 6 No.7 1958

Picture Credits

1) Drawing of a Mesolithic hunting scene. © *Museum of London*
2) Reconstruction of an early Mesolithic settlement, based on finds from The Nab Head, Pembrokeshire. © *National Museum of Wales*
3) The Coldharbour settlement 1880 Middlesex OS Map XX16 25" to a mile. *Courtesy of Richmond upon Thames Local Studies Library & Archive*
4) Hoe or Mattock found near Cold Harbour - *Courtesy of David Field*
5) Hand axe fitted to a shaft – *Courtesy of The Museum of Richmond*
6) Distribution of Mesolithic core tools in West of London - *Courtesy of David Field*
7) Mesolithic Mace Head found by A Bott at the Thames foreshore – *Courtesy of The Museum of Richmond*
8) Mesolithic Flint adze found near Coldharbour. *Courtesy of the Museum of Richmond*
9) Aerial picture of the United Kingdom.
10) A reconstruction drawing of a Mesolithic wolf, which was created in 1995 by artist Derek Lucas. © *Museum of London*
11) A reconstruction drawing of a Mesolithic wild boar, which was created in 1995 by artist Derek Lucas. © *Museum of London*
12) A reconstruction drawing of a Mesolithic wild horse, which was created in 1995 by artist Derek Lucas. © *Museum of London*

Chapter Five. Deferred Settlement

Sources of Information

1) Field D. Ham: The Edwards Collection Surrey Archaeological Collection Volume 74 (1983) 169-184
2) www.bbc.co.uk/history/ british/timeline/neolithic
3) The Archaeology of the Gravel Terraces Early Prehistory to 1500BC. Oxford Archaeology
4) Ross C & Clark J London -The Illustrated History/Penguin Books 2011
5) Merriman N. - Prehistoric London
6) R.Adkins and R. Jackson *Neolithic Stone and Flint Axes from the River Thames; an illustrated Corpus,* British Museum Occasional Paper no. 1 (1978)
7) Johnson & Wright: Neolithic man in North East Surrey 1903.
8) Elias Allen in 1630 produced a map of the Park showing a mound with a large tree on top. (PRO/MPE 986)
9) E. Jesse: Gleanings in Natural History 1835 245-6
10) John Beighton: Richmond Park, it's natural resources published in The Leisure Hour September 1887 page 618.
11) Dr Tom Greeves; Richmond Park – A report on the archaeology of an area near Ham Gate 1990 (Unpublished typescript)
12) Dr Tom Greeves; Richmond Park, London archaeological survey 1992 (Unpublished typescript)
13) Kingston Museum Accession 1117/GLSMR 0209764

Picture Credits

1) Representation of an auroch hunt during the Neolithic period. © *Museum of London*
2) Neolithic flint axe from Isabella plantation © *Museum of London*
3) Representation of tree felling during the Neolithic period. © *Museum of London*
4) Photo of an auroch's skull. *Courtesy of Professor Danielle Schreve and the Department of Geography, Royal Holloway University of London.*
5) Photo of a Leaf shaped arrowhead found at Walkers Market Garden. *Courtesy of Richmond Museum*
6) A reconstruction drawing of a Neolithic sheep, which was created in 1995 by artist Derek Lucas. © *Museum of London*
7) A reconstruction drawing of a Neolithic goat, which was created in 1995 by artist Derek Lucas. © *Museum of London*

8) The 1630 map of Richmond Park made by Elias Allen. *Courtesy of Public Records Office, Kew.*

9) Brayley E.W (1850) A Topographical History of Surrey. Vol 3. Map by R.B.Ede on page 65. *Courtesy of Richmond upon Thames Local Studies Library & Archive.*

10) Map showing the location of Barrow features identified by Dr. Tom Greeves created by Gordon Elsden

11) Two photographs of the Long Barrow identified by Dr. Tom Greeves taken by Gordon Elsden

12) Sunset from the top of the Terrace – Gordon Elsden

Chapter Six. Metal Divides

Sources of Information

1) Field D. - Ham: The Edwards Collection
2) Ross C & Clark J London -The Illustrated History/Penguin Books 2011
3) Bradley Richard: The Prehistory of Britain and Ireland/ Cambridge University Press 2007
4) Field D. - "Ham" The Edwards Collection" Surrey Archaeological Collect 74 (1983) 169-184
5) Evidence for Bronze age settlement on Coombe Warren, Kingston Hill by D. Field & S. Needham
6) Merriman Nick – Prehistoric London HMSO 1990
7) Monumenta Britannica edited by Fowles c 1981, 270-71
8) Dr Tom Greeves; Richmond Park, London archaeological survey 1992 (Unpublished typescript)
9) Cowie R. - Prehistoric Twickenham (including Ham Fields) London Archaeologist vol 9 no. 9
10) S Needham and C Burgess "The late Bronze age in the lower Thames Valley; the metalwork evidence" in J Barrett and R Bradley (eds)
11) http://www.smithsonianmag.com/history/
12) Antiquities from the Middle Thames 1929 - G.F.Lawrence Page 75-6

Picture Credits

1) Bronze Age sword found in the Thames. *By permission of Kingston Museum and Heritage Service.*

2) Bronze Age beaker found in Coldharbour. *Courtesy of the Museum of Richmond.*

3) Photos of two barbed and tangled arrowheads. ©*Museum of London*

4) Copper ingot. *By permission of Kingston Museum and Heritage Service*

5) Bronze Age Sword. ©*Museum of London*

6) Aubrey's comment on the Ham Heath shown in 'Monumenta Britannica' edited by Fowles c 1981, 270-71

7) A modern day photo showing the elevated path running from Ham Common woods by Gordon Elsden

8) Lidar Survey showing Ham Common

9) Map of Ham produced by Gordon Elsden

10) Funerary Rites on the bank of the Thames. © *Museum of Londo1*

11) Ceramic Collared urn - DSC F0645 (62.45) © *Museum of London*

12) Ceramic Collared urn - DSC F0663 (66.31/1) © *Museum of London*

13) Damaged Bronze Age spearheads. *By permission of Kingston Museum and Heritage Service*

14) Photo of Stoney Jack.

15) Bronze Dirk. © *The Trustees of the British Museum*

16) Bronze Spear Butt. © *The Trustees of the British Museum*

Chapter Seven. The Influence of Rome

Sources of Information

1) Bradley Richard: The Prehistory of Britain and Ireland/ Cambridge University Press 2007
2) Sargent Andrew -The Story of the Thames
3) Merriman Nick – Prehistoric London HMSO 1990
4) Field D. "Ham" The Edwards Collection" Surrey Archaeological Collect 74 (1983) 169-184
5) Cowie Robert - Prehistoric Twickenham (including Ham Fields)
6) Rendall Rosemary: Iron Age and Roman pottery sherds from Richmond Park Surrey Archaeological Collections Vol 74 1983.
7) Cunliffe Barry - Iron Age Britain
8) James Dr Simon:
   www.bbc.co.uk/history/ancient/british_prehistory/peoples
9) www.bbc.co.uk/history/ancient/british_prehistory/ironage
10) www.britishmuseum.org/explore/online_tours/britain/people-in-iron-age
11) http://www.wimbledonmuseum.org.uk/index.php/on-view/early-wimble don/pre-history 11/2015

12) Dr Tom Greeves; Richmond Park, London archaeological survey 1992 (Unpublished typescript)
13) Cunliffe Barry - Britain Begins (page 26)
14) Book IV Chapter 5 Strabo - Geography published in Vol. II of the Loeb Classical Library edition, 1923
15) Kent John: 'The London area in the Late Iron Age: An interpretation of the earliest coins' in the following volume: Collectanea Londiniensia: Studies in London archaeology and history presented to Ralph Merrifield, J Bird, H Chapman and J Clark (eds), London & Middx Arch Soc Special Paper 2 (1978), 53-58.
16) Caesar Julius - 'The Gallic War' translated by T. Rice Holmes. Book V
17) Caesar Julius - 'The Gallic War' Book V Chapter 16
18) Caesar Julius - 'The Gallic War' Book V Chapters 17–19
19) Caesar Julius - 'The Gallic War' Book V Chapter 18
20) Caesar Julius - 'The Gallic War' Book V Chapter 21

Picture Credits

1) Iron Age settlement model.
   By permission of Kingston Museum and Heritage Service
2) Adapted from a drawing in Ham: The Edwards Collection by David Field.
3) Image of an Iron age coin ©*Museum of London*
4) Representation of an Iron Age homestead – Thanks to Natalie Mabelis
5) Painting by Julian Cross, © *Wessex Archaeology.*
6) Representation of a Loom - Thanks to Natalie Mabelis
7) Artistic impression of a rotary quern stone.
8) Map marked up by Gordon Elsden
9) Photo of Broomfield Hill taken by Gordon Elsden
10) The Triumphs of Caesar – The captives library *Royal Collection Trust |* © *Her Majesty Queen Elizabeth II 2014*
11) Iron Age Chariot English Heritage © *English Heritage*
12) Tribal feast English Heritage © *English Heritage*
13) Artistic impression of a Sling shot
14) Sling shot boys © *Paul Birkbeck. Source: English Heritage*
15) The Battersea Shield © *The Trustees of the British Museum*
16) The Romans arrive in Britain - Picture by Angus McBride & Concord Publishing

17) Advancing Roman Infantry
18) Roman troops crossing the Thames. *Courtesy of Look and Learn*
19) Artistic impression of a Roman scout
20) Caesar leaving Britain to its destiny. *Courtesy of Look and Learn*

Chapter Eight. The Pax Romana

Sources of Information

1) Ham: The Edwards Collection Volume LXXIV 1983 Surrey Archaeological Collection by David Field
2) Finds in British Museum - Monument No. 398038 Greater London Authority
3) SMR Number MLO103886 - Roman finds in Ham Lands
4) That Famous Place" – A History of Kingston Upon Thames by Shaan Butters
5) The Romans who shaped Britain by Sam Moorhead and David Stuttard
6) http://www.wimbledonmuseum.org.uk/index.php/on-view/early-wimbledon /pre-history 11/2015
7) The Story of the Thames - Andrew Sargent.
8) The Romano British period in Surrey by. D.G. Bird
9) Dr Tom Greeves; Richmond Park, London archaeological survey 1992 (Unpublished typescript)

Picture Credits

1) Ring necked flagon found in Coldharbour.
   Courtesy of the Museum of Richmond.
2) A complete ring necked flagon on display in the Museum of London © *Museum of London.*
3) Picture of a cinerary urn –© Museum of London
4) Advancing Roman infantry encountering British Warriors.
   © *Paul Birkbeck. Source: English Heritage*
5) Picture of Boudicca – *Courtesy of Look and learn*
6) Two Photos of Dr. Tom Greeves and the ancient track running through Richmond Park by Gordon Elsden

Chapter Nine. A Saxon Shore

Sources of Information

1) Rob Poulton: Saxon Surrey in The Archaeology of Surrey to 1540 Edited by Joanna Bird and DG Bird (Page 220: 24)
2) Zosimus, "Historia Nova"
3) Robert Cowie & Charlotte Harding - Saxon Settlement and Economy from The Dark Ages to Domesday, in the Archaeology of greater London(ed MOLAS) Surveys and Handbooks 171-98 London 2000
4) Anglo Saxon and Norse Poems ; Translated by N Kershaw 1922 http://www.archive.org/stream/anglosaxonnorsep00chadrich#page/54/mode/2up
5) The Anglo-Saxon Chronicle, though created in the 9th Century provides a year-by-year account dating from AD 449 of all the major events during the Saxon period. It documents the rise and fall of the Kings and Bishops and the important battles of the period. http://omacl.org/Anglo/part1.html (Followed by part 2, part 3, part 4....)
6) Robert Cowie and Lyn Blackmore - Early and Middle Saxon rural settlement in the London region. MOLAS Monograph 41 Museum of London
7) GLSMR 021046 – ML0138
8) J.N.L Myres – A Corpus of Anglo Saxon Pottery of the pagan period. 1,247, and 2, fig 201:1044). 1977,
9) Notes and sketches made by Hope Taylor and now stored in RCAHM Edinburgh HT/37/1
10) Urwin A.C.B Twickenham before 704AD Borough of Twickenham Local History Society Paper Number 45 1980
11) Shaan Butters That Famous Place – A History of Kingston Upon Thames. KU Press 2013
12) The account of the abbey in the Chertsey chartulary preserved among the Cott. MS. Vitel. A. xiii. f.
13) Charles D. Warren – History of St Peter's Church. 1938
14) London, British Library, Cotton Vitellius A.XIII S 1181 http://www.esawyer.org.uk/charter/1181.html
15) http://www.petershamvillage.org/history.html
16) Historic England - Monument No. 398038
17) C.E. Vulliamy, The Archaelogy of Middlesex and London 1930 (page 230)
18) Proceedings of the Society of Antiquaries of London Volume 24 Page 327 – 329 1912
19) http://oldenglishteaching.arts.gla.ac.uk
20) John Cloake - The Early History of Ham (page 1) Richmond Local History
21) Anglo Saxon Charter www.esawyer.org.uk/charter
22) http://www.allsaintskingston.co.uk/heritage/timeline
23) John Morris "Anglo Saxon Surrey", The Gazetteer. P 144, Surrey AC Vol 61
24) Dr Tom Greeves; Richmond Park, London archaeological survey 1992 (Unpublished typescript) Section 5.3
25) Bede - A History of the English Church and People, Book II Chapter 13 AD 731

Picture Credits

1) Artistic impression of Roman London left to decay taken from an Edwardian postcard showing Roman ruins at Virginia Water.
2) Saxons entering deserted London. Illustration for Story of the British Nation (Hutchinson, c 1920). *Courtesy of Look and Learn*
3) Reconstruction of an early Saxon settlement. *Courtesy of the Museum of Richmond.*
4) A 5th Century carinated pedestal bowl from a drawing in "A Corpus of Anglo-Saxon pottery of the Pagan Period by J.N.L. Myres Volume 2.
5) Argonne ware bowl drawing © *MOLA*
6) Picture of a shard of Argonne red ware. *reproduced by permission of Bingham Heritage Trails Association http://www.binghamheritage.org.uk*
7) Other decorated vessels drawings © *MOLA*
8) Simple jars drawings © *MOLA*
9) Larger jars drawings © *MOLA*
10) Cups or smaller bowls © *MOLA*
11) A Saxon loom drawn by S.J Plunkett
12) A Saxon Helmet © *The Trustees of the British Museum*
13) Bede's Sparrow - © *Carrie Wild 2010*
14) Picture of a Saxon cross by Gordon Elsden
15) Picture of a chaff Tempered Saxon urn - Gordon Elsden
16) Picture of a Saxon spear. *Courtesy of St Albans Museum*
17) A Saxon sword found in a grave at Ham © *The Trustees of the British Museum*
18) Drawing of a Saxon shield boss found at Ham shown in Proceedings of the Society of Antiquaries of London 1912 Page 329
19) The Saxon Shield Wall Illustration by www.davidhobbsillustration.com

20) An Anglo Saxon gold pendant found in a grave at Ham © *The Trustees of the British Museum.*

21) The Sandstone block reputed to be the Coronation Stone – Photo by Gordon Elsden

22) A Saxon Village fair. *Courtesy of Look and Learn*

23) Viking Longships making their way up the Thames drawn by Ken Cooper

24) Chertsey Abbey sacked by the Vikings

25) Map showing Wessex, Mercia and The Danelaw in 878. Produced by Hel-hama -. Licensed under CC BY-SA 3.0

26) Picture of a loomstone. *Courtesy of Surrey Archaeological Society, Castle Arch.*

27) Art in Nature in Richmond Park at the site of a Middle Saxon settlement – Gordon Elsden

28) Image of King Athlelstan. c.895-939. Illuminated manuscript from Bede's Life of St Cuthbert, c.930. A public domain work of art

29) A Viking Raid © Brian Palmer

30) A portrait of Ethelred the Unready. Ethelred in an early thirteenth-century copy of the Abingdon Chronicle. A public domain work of art.

31) Sketch Map of Kingston Hundred. This map is an illustration from The Victoria History of the County of Surrey, Volume 3, page 481 edited by H.E. Malden

Chapter Ten. Lords of the Manor

Sources of Information

1) Robert Bartlett - J.M. Roberts, ed. *England Under the Norman and Angevin 2000*

2) Michael Wood - *The Domesday Quest.* London: BBC (1985)

3) The Great Domesday Book Folio 32V Ref E31/2/1/954 The National Archives Kew http://discovery.nationalarchives.gov.uk/details/r/D7300328

4) John Cloake – The Early History of Ham: Richmond Local History Society Journals No. 11 May 1990 & No. 12 May 1991)

5) Shaan Butters That Famous Place – A History of Kingston Upon Thames. KU Press 2013

6) Rev Owen Manning – The History and Antiquities of the County of Surrey 1804 - Volume 1 Pages 359

7) The Victoria History of the County of Surrey Volume 3

8) Gillian Kenny- The Heiress as Fortune-Maker and Widow in Thirteenth-Century Anglo-Norman Ireland http://www.ucd.ie/pages/97/kenny.html

9) Marc Morris - Edward I – A Great and Terrible King. This was a very useful reference for building the picture of the lives of Robert Burnell and Sir Otto de Grandison

10.) Westminster Abbey Website http://www.westminster-abbey.org/our-history/royals/edward-i-and-eleanor-of-castile

11) Barney Sloane – The Black Death in London; 2011

12) Demolition records for the Secrett's farm dated June 1958 located at Surrey History Centre

13) Fred S. Thacker - The Thames Highway Volume II Locks and Weirs Page 455.

14) Customs of the Manor of Ham held at Surrey History centre SHS 2337/7/1

15) John Cloake – The Origin of the Ham House Grounds. Richmond Local History Society Journal No.22 May 2001

16) Evelyn Pritchard – The Ham Street Bend and the Great Barn of Ham. Richmond Local History Society Journal No.20 May 1999

17) Raymond Gill – Richmond Park in the 17th century Barnes and Mortlake History Society Occasional Paper Number 4. 1990

18) Filkins Notes held at Richmond Local Studies Centre

19) John Cloake The Robin Hood Lands, the Hamlet of Hatch and the Manor of Kingston Canbury. Richmond Local History Society Journal

20) Dr Tom Greeves; Richmond Park, London Archaeological Survey 1992 (Unpublished typescript)

Picture Credits

1) Pictures of Norman soldiers advancing through Britain and a Norman shield wall after the conquest. Gordon Elsden

2) King William confronting his Barons – Gordon Elsden

3) The entry for Petersham in the 1086 Domesday Book. *Courtesy of The National Archives Kew*

4) The penance of King Henry II. Public Domain Image

5) A 13th Century image of Maurice de Creon. Public domain image

6) King John signing the Magna Carta. © *The British Library*

7) A 14th Century Manuscript image of King Edward I and Queen Eleanor. Public Domain image.

8) Robert Burnell. Public Domain Image

9) Image of Sir Otto de Grandison on the base of the tomb of Queen Eleanor. A reconstruction drawing by E Tristram of base painting on the tomb. *Courtesy of Dean & Chapter of Westminster Abbey.*

10) Siege of Acre. Public domain image11.)
The Four Horsemen of the Apocalypse. Public Domain Image
12) The Dance Macabre. Public domain image
13) Brass rubbing of Sir Nicholas Burnell
© *Ashmolean Museum, University of Oxford*
14) King Henry V at the Battle of Agincourt, 1415, Gilbert, John (1817-97) / Atkinson Art Gallery, Southport, Lancashire, UK / Bridgeman Images.
15) OS 1913 Map of Ham Surrey VI 8
16) Photo of Ham Manor Farm House circa 1870 *(Reproduced by permission of Surrey History Centre) (SHC)*
17) Photo of Ham Manor Farm Tithe Barn taken in 1956 as part of the Antiquities of Surrey project *(Reproduced by permission of Surrey History Centre)*
18) Manor Farm Barn c 1940 Drawing made by John Sanderson in 1940 as part of the Recording Britain Collection. © *Victoria and Albert Museum, London*
19) Photos of the Ham Manor Farm House taken in 1956 & 1957 as part of the Antiquities of Surrey project (Reproduced by permission of SHC)
20a) Picture of Edward IV. Public Domain Image
20b) Picture of Elizabeth Woodville. Public Domain Image
21) Copyright Sean Twiddy. Image provided here for educational purposes and to aquaint new viewers with Twiddy's work.
22) Photos of Ham House – Gordon Elsden
23) The Elias Allen map of 1630. Courtesy of Kew Public Records Office. Work 32/687
24) The Surveyed map of the land to be contained within the new hunting Park by Nicholas Lane in 1632.
Courtesy of Kew Public Records Office. Work 32/687
25) Hartleton Farm shown on the Elias Allen map of 1630
Courtesy of Kew Public Records Office. (MPE 1/986)
26a) Photoshop image of Cromwell inspecting his army on Ham Common – Gordon Elsden
26) Loanes House shown on the Nicholas Lane map of 1632.
Courtesy of Kew Public Records Office. Work 32/687 PRO
27) Portrait of the Duke and Duchess of Lauderdale by Sir Peter Lely.
© *National Trust*
28) Photo of the former Almshouse on Ham Parade – Gordon Elsden
29) Mediaeval ridge and furrow near to Ham Gate as shown on a Lidar survey of the Park
30) Mediaeval Road passing through Richmond Park –
Courtesy of Dr. Tom Greeves

Chapter Eleven. The Transformation of Rural Ham

Sources of Information

1) Evelyn Pritchard – Early Victorian Ham 1840-1860
2) The Ham River Grit Company & The Ham Lands - Arcadian Times, May 7th 2011
3) Eric Parker – Highways and Byways in Surrey 1925

Picture Credits

1) Ham Street - the river end. Drawing made by John Sanderson in 1940 as part of the Recording Britain Collection. © Victoria and Albert Museum, London
2) Edge of Manor Farm, Ham Street. Drawing made by John Sanderson in 1940 as part of the Recording Britain Collection.
© *Victoria and Albert Museum, London*
3) The Greenwoods in Lammas Lands, Ham.
Courtesy of Richmond upon Thames Local Studies Library & Archive
4) 1944 RAF Sortie aerial photograph of Ham © *English Heritage*
5) Cows from Ham Manor Farm passing Ham House stables in Ham Street. Drawing made by John Sanderson in 1940 as part of the Recording Britain Collection. © *Victoria and Albert Museum, London*
6) Ham Riverside Lands – *Courtesy of Sir David Williams*
7) Ham Common at sunrise – Gordon Elsden
8) Postcard of Ham Common Pond c1900
Courtesy of Richmond upon Thames Local Studies Library & Archive
9) Ham Common Pond – Gordon Elsden
10) Latchmere Brook – Gordon Elsden
11) Sudbrook – Gordon Elsden
12) Ham Gate Pond- Gordon Elsden
13) Ham Dip Pond – Gordon Elsden
14) Pen Ponds – Gordon Elsden
15) Attenborough Watering Hole – Gordon Elsden
16) Stags grazing close to Attenborough Watering Hole – Gordon Elsden
17) Having fun in Richmond Park – Gordon Elsden

Chapter Twelve. Legacy

Picture Credits

1) Enjoying the natural landscape in the ancient park of Ham – Gordon Elsden

Index

Maps

Index

Gordon Elsden

Gordon was raised within the Parish of Ham, attending local junior and secondary schools but gaining an important part of his education while roaming the vast landscape of Richmond Park, Ham Common and playing on the fringes and on occasions in the River Thames.

After graduating from Loughborough University with a degree in Economics and Mathematics he left these shores to take up a Colonial Post as an Inspector in the Royal Hong Kong Police Force. These were exciting times with demanding postings that included working as a Detective Inspector in the dynamic City district of Tsim Sha Tsui and as a Platoon Commander of an anti riot platoon in the more rural New Territories.

With the imminent handover of Hong Kong, Gordon returned to the UK to begin a new career in International Business which took him all around the World but ultimately focused him on the developing markets of China and the Far East. He now has a business and office in the concentrated urban environment of Shanghai and a home in Ham, and spends much time travelling between the two locations.

His journey has taken him to the extremes of rapidly changing densely populated urban cities, the highest mountain ranges in the world and nomadic landscapes in the far west of China and Central Asia that have changed little in a thousand years.

This has given Gordon a greater appreciation of the settled and secure environment of Ham and a wonderful natural landscape embraced by the River Thames only a short walking distance from his home. It also prompted him to look a little closer and ask a few questions.

Armed with a greater understanding of the special nature of Ham, Gordon was motivated to write this book and to bring alive once more the story of Ham's long forgotten and fascinating past.